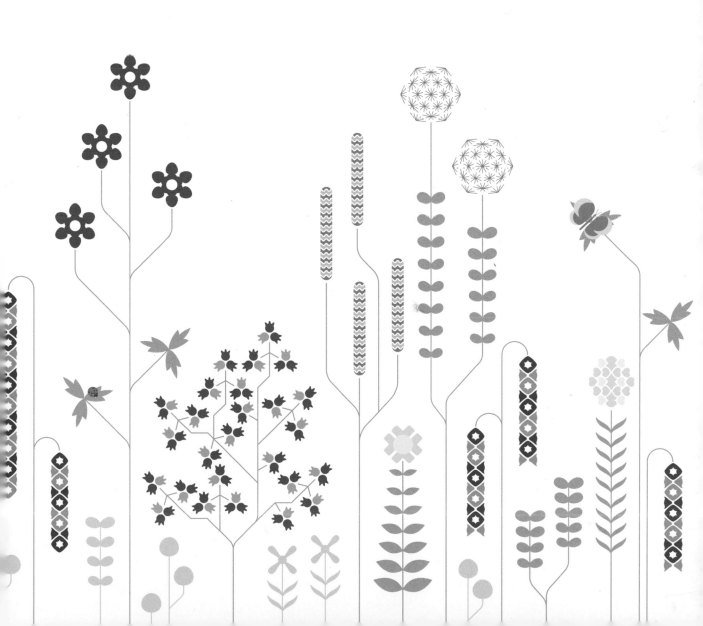

SNOG™
healthy treats
cookbook

SNOG™
healthy treats
cookbook

RYLAND
PETERS
& SMALL

LONDON NEW YORK

♥ This book is dedicated to the pursuit of healthy eating and encouraging our physical, mental and spiritual well-being.

Recipe developers and writers
Mariana Velasquez and Cristina Archila

Photography Kate Whitaker

**Design, Photographic Art Direction
and Prop Styling** Steve Painter
Senior Commissioning Editor Julia Charles
Head of Production Patricia Harrington
Art Director Leslie Harrington
Publishing Director Alison Starling

Food Stylist Lucy McKelvie
Illustration Akira Chatani
Indexer Hilary Bird

**Snog corporate branding and company
graphic design** ICO Design

First published in 2011
by Ryland Peters & Small
20–21 Jockey's Fields
London WC1R 4BW
and
Ryland Peters & Small, Inc.
519 Broadway, 5th Floor
New York, NY10012
www.rylandpeters.com

10 9 8 7 6 5 4 3 2 1

Text © Pablo Uribe 2011
Design and commissioned photography
© Ryland Peters & Small 2011
Photographs on pages 6 and 15
© Fernando Manoso-Borgas, ICO Design

Printed in China

ISBN: 978 1 84975 080 6

A CIP record for this book is available from the British Library.

US Library of Congress cataloging-in-publication data has been applied for.

Notes
• Agave nectar is widely available in health food stores and larger supermarkets. However, if you experience difficulty sourcing it, it can also be found at the following online stores:
UK
www.goodnessdirect.co.uk
www.groovyfood.co.uk
US
www.organicdirect.com
www.globalgoods.com

• All spoon measurements are level, unless otherwise specified.
• Eggs are medium unless otherwise specified and organic free-range eggs are strongly recommended.
• Ovens should be preheated to the specified temperature. Recipes in this book were tested using a regular oven. If using a fan-assisted oven, follow the manufacturer's instructions for adjusting temperatures.
• When a recipe calls for the grated zest/peel of citrus fruit, buy unwaxed fruit and wash it well before using.

contents

all about Snog

Snog was born out of our passion for healthy eating. Having had Tinto, a coffee house in leafy Fulham in London since 2000, we wanted to open a new type of shop. After meeting up with our friend Lorraine, a nutritionist, we both mentioned how tired we felt after having a meal. She suggested it could be gluten related and suggested we gave up gluten for a month. It was hard as a lot of the foods we eat contain gluten – pasta, pizza, some soups, muffins and granola, for example – but we both decided to give it a go. After a month we both felt amazing. Our energy levels had increased and we felt very upbeat. We had been converted, having been able to experience first hand how what you eat defines the way you feel. We knew then that our next venture would be about healthy treats.

On our frequent trips to Miami, we would have my (Pablo's) sister Xandy over for dinner and she would always make the same simple dessert. She would bring all the ingredients and right after dinner she would prepare Greek yogurt topped with fresh fruits, mint leaves, dates and walnuts all drizzled with agave nectar. Little did we know then that this would be the inspiration for the Snog you buy in our shops. In 2007 when we started seeing frozen yogurt shops open up in the US we decided to bring the concept over to London. We were disappointed when we found out that the main ingredient in frozen yogurt was sugar. We remembered Xandy's yogurt with agave nectar and took this as the starting point for our recipe.

We then embarked on finding a name and decided to call on a friend, Niall from ICO Design, to help us. We briefed his studio team and Snog as a brand was born. Having had an architecture practice in Miami and London, designing for the likes of Calvin Klein, we wanted the retail experience to be captivating. We teamed up with Dominic from Cinimod Studio to help us with the interior design and lighting and the design for the first shop came about.

Finding a location was difficult. There were no frozen yogurt shops in London and landlords were not keen on the idea. We finally opened our first shop in South Kensington and from the day we opened it was a success. People were obviously looking for healthy treats and the environment we had created was well loved too. We were inspired by a perfect British summer's day. Our floor is a grass print, there are rolling clouds in the ceiling, the walls have prints of wild flowers and the seats are Shitake Stools by Marcel Wanders placed around outdoor garden-inspired tables. We then knew London was ready for more shops. We are fond of Soho's vibrancy and mix so we chose to open our second shop there. This time it was much easier to convince the landlords. We then decided to open in Westfield White City, a great new mall in West London. Then Covent Garden came along, then a pop-up in Liberty of London and then King's Road, Chelsea. Our first international shop was in Dubai. It get's so hot in the Middle East we knew it would be a good fit. The shops are about the customer experience and have been our live billboards. We have done no marketing and word of mouth has been our best advocate. We strive to entertain and give consumers a healthy product in a fun, well-designed space. We are doing great work with people at the Royal College of Art. Tomas Alonso, a graduate, designed our limited edition spoons you get with a Snog Special. James Tooze, also a student there, designed our travelling pop-up which had Liberty of London as its first home, and we have more exciting projects in the pipeline. We are striving to keep our customers engaged in order to keep Snog relevant.

The aim of this book is to bring to your home recipes that are good for you, easy to make and tasty. We teamed up with Mariana Velásquez and Cristina Archila, both Colombian born. Mariana has worked with various magazines in the US like *Eating Well*, *Saveur* and *Bon Appetit*. Cristina's passion is raw food and nutrition and she is permanently researching well-being and healing practices among different cultures. We all hope you will enjoy learning more about Snog, following our vibrant recipes and reaping the benefits of making healthy eating choices every day.

Pablo Uribe & Rob Baines

why eat Snog healthy treats?

When we eat wholesome fresh ingredients, our bodies becomes leaner, our skin glows and our energy levels increase. Our whole lifestyle shifts and ultimately becomes healthier. These food choices are powerful decisions that dictate what we look like and how we feel. Taking responsibility for how we nourish ourselves goes far beyond food; it's who we are; it's how we relate to the planet. Ultimately, if food keeps us alive, shouldn't we consume lively foods?

Lively foods are whole, natural foods that contain valuable nutrients and support sustainability. As we consume these foods we enable our bodies to assimilate more nutrients and eliminate proper waste. Our bodies understand the composition of whole, natural foods and benefit from them when eaten in balanced amounts. The closer an ingredient remains to its pure and natural form, the more beneficial it will be for all of us. Ultimately, the origin, handling and quality of our food matters a great deal. It is our own responsibility to relate to the food we eat with greater consciousness. We need to stay informed about healthy and sustainable options. Choosing healthier foods should not mean sacrificing flavour in any way. It may mean exploring, planning or preparing foods with a bit more diligence, but that's a small task in return for optimal health, well-being and longevity.

This shift towards a healthier lifestyle will expand awareness in many aspects of our lives. Inevitably we develop interest in the stories behind our food, its origins and how it affects all of us. It becomes clear why we need to treat food with greater significance. It is our very own preventive medicine and it dictates the quality of our life. It is our vital energy source and we have the privilege of making the 'best' possible choice every time. Making the 'best' choice is crucial when it comes to eating sweet treats. Most of us love them, they are a celebration of life. Treats are a special delight; they should nourish our body and satisfy our soul. Choosing healthy treats will benefit our organs, our mind and our planet. May the recipes in this book inspire you to get adventurous and prepare many delicious healthy treats: food that we love and that loves us back.

what is agave nectar?

Agave nectar is a natural sweet alternative for people with sugar sensitivities and for those watching their nutrition. The agave plant is considered sacred in its native Central America, where its golden liquid is believed to purify the body and soul. Agave nectar is about 90 percent fructose and 10 percent glucose. This natural fructose has the lowest Glycaemic Index value (GI) of any sweetener (between 25 and 50 – refined sugar notches up a massive 92). This means that agave nectar will not raise our blood sugar levels and overstimulate the production of insulin. This fructose-rich nectar has a neutral, yet concentrated sweetness that makes it ideal for preparing wholesome natural recipes. Agave nectar comes in light, amber and dark

varieties and is available from healthfood stores and some larger supermarkets. Its flavour intensifies with the colour and I would recommend using light agave nectar for the recipes in this book. There are different ways to produce agave nectar and it is important to choose a good-quality, organic, fair-trade brand. Look for one that has not been boiled, altered and stripped of its nutrients. The purest agave nectar will be labelled 'raw agave nectar' and is derived from the sap collected when the plant's flower has been cut off. This nectar contains iron, calcium, potassium and magnesium. Of course, agave nectar, like all sweeteners, should be consumed in moderation.

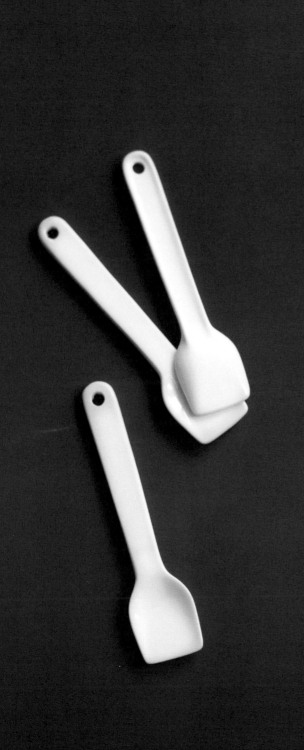

frozen treats

Snog pure frozen yogurt

We developed these recipes for the home, looking to achieve the tangy, fresh and clean tasting qualities of our frozen yogurt by using some of the same basic natural ingredients. At our shops we use specialized commercial equipment that imparts the right amount of air and maintains the perfect temperature for smoothness.

natural

720 ml / 3 cups plain Greek yogurt (0% fat)

360 ml / 1½ cups organic low-fat milk

120 ml / ½ cup agave nectar

2 teaspoons freshly squeezed lemon juice

an ice cream maker (optional)

Makes about 1.4 litres / 1.5 quarts

Whisk together the yogurt, milk, agave nectar and lemon juice in a large bowl. Transfer to the bowl of an ice cream maker and churn according to the manufacturer's directions, until creamy and smooth. If you do not have an ice cream maker, pour the mixture into a freezerproof container. Put on the lid and place in the freezer. After about 45 minutes check the mixture. As it starts to freeze around the edges beat vigorously with a fork, whisk, electric hand mixer or spatula to break up the ice crystals. Repeat periodically until the mixture is frozen, about 2–3 hours.

chocolate

Follow the recipe for Natural Pure Frozen Yogurt (see above), whisking in 3 tablespoons of sifted good-quality unsweetened cocoa powder (ideally Italian) before freezing.

green tea

Follow the recipe for Natural Pure Frozen Yogurt (see above), whisking in 1 tablespoon of green matcha tea powder before freezing.

♥ **yogurt** is a wonderful source of protein, calcium and potassium. It is rich in probiotics, the friendly micro-organisms that strengthen our immune systems and promote healthy digestion. Yogurt is a fermented food that ranks among the healthiest treats available.

♥ **green tea** is a potent antioxidant. It is very effective in reducing the levels of LDL 'bad' cholesterol, fighting cancer and repairing cell damage. Green tea contains theanine, a 'feel-good' substance that improves mood and relaxation. This aids the brain in the release of dopamine, which regulates pleasure, calmness and a sense of well-being.

♥ **chocolate** is loaded with flavonols and antioxidants. It is important to consume the best quality of chocolate – dark chocolate with a high cocoa content, to receive its benefits. Chocolate helps maintain cardiovascular health and regulates blood pressure by modulating the nitric oxide in our bodies.

pomegranate and vanilla pod frozen yogurt

Pomegranate molasses is a great ingredient. It contains no added sugar and its flavour is strong and sharp. A little goes a long way and it's perfect for drizzling.

120 ml / ½ cup organic low-fat milk

1 vanilla pod / bean or 2 teaspoons vanilla extract

180 ml / ¾ cup unsweetened pomegranate juice

840 ml / 3½ cups plain Greek yogurt (0% fat)

160 ml / ⅔ cup agave nectar

2 tablespoons pomegranate molasses

pomegranate drizzle (optional)

480 ml / 2 cups pomegranate juice

an ice cream maker (optional)

Makes about 1 litre / quart

Put the milk in a small saucepan set over medium heat. Split the vanilla pod in half lengthways and use the tip of the knife to scrape the seeds into the milk and add the pod. Bring the milk to a simmer, cover and remove from the heat. Let stand for about 10–15 minutes, so that the vanilla infuses the milk with flavour. Remove the vanilla pod and allow the milk to cool.

Put the pomegranate juice, yogurt, agave nectar and pomegranate molasses in a large bowl. Stir in the vanilla-infused milk and refrigerate until the mixture is very cold.

Transfer to the bowl of an ice cream maker and churn according to the manufacturer's directions, until creamy and smooth. If you do not have an ice cream maker, pour the mixture into a freezerproof container. Put on the lid and place in the freezer. After about 45 minutes check the mixture. As it starts to freeze around the edges beat vigorously with a fork, whisk, electric hand-held mixer or spatula to break up the ice crystals. Repeat periodically until the mixture is frozen, about 2–3 hours.

To make the pomegranate drizzle, put the pomegranate juice in a small saucepan and set over medium/high heat. Bring to the boil and then reduce the heat to medium/low and simmer for 35–40 minutes, until reduced to about 120 ml / ½ cup. Chill and drizzle over scoops of the frozen yogurt just before serving.

❤ **pomegranates** have very potent antioxidants that help keep us young, fight heart disease and prevent cancer. They are a good source of vitamins B and C, calcium and phosphorous. Pomegranate juice helps maintain healthy arteries, reduces the levels of LDL 'bad' cholesterol and promotes prostate health.

apricot cardamom frozen yogurt with pistachio swirl

Fresh apricots are a delicious summer treat and using them in all ways possible is a must! Here the exotic Middle Eastern flavours of cardamom and pistachios evoke a Persian garden in bloom.

360 ml / 1½ cups vanilla-flavoured low-fat yogurt

240 ml / 1 cup fat-free buttermilk

120 ml / ½ cup apricot nectar (see note on page 122)

1 tablespoon freshly squeezed lemon juice

140 g / ¾ cup diced fresh apricots

60 ml / ¼ cup agave nectar

⅛ teaspoon ground cardamom (alternatively use 2–3 cardamom pods, split them, scoop out the seeds and crush finely)

3 tablespoons chopped toasted pistachios

an ice cream maker (optional)

Makes 1.4 litres / 1.5 quarts

Put the yogurt, buttermilk, apricot nectar, lemon juice and apricots in a large bowl and stir to combine. Transfer the mixture to the bowl of an ice cream maker and churn according to the manufacturer's directions, until creamy and smooth. If you do not have an ice cream maker, pour the mixture into a freezerproof container. Put on the lid and place in the freezer. After about 45 minutes check the mixture. As it starts to freeze around the edges beat vigorously with a fork, whisk, electric hand-held mixer or spatula to break up the ice crystals. Repeat periodically until the mixture is frozen, about 4 hours.

Stir together the agave nectar and cardamom powder or crushed cardamom seeds in a small bowl and set aside.

Take the frozen yogurt out of the freezer and allow it to soften slightly. Sprinkle the toasted pistachios over the top and pour the agave nectar and cardamom mixture into the frozen yogurt. Using a rubber spatula make a few strokes to partially mix it in. Return to the freezer until ready to serve.

❤ **pistachio nuts** are loaded with heart-healthy monounsaturated fat and antioxidant power. They contain vitamin E, which boosts the immune system and are rich in magnesium, copper, manganese and vitamin B6. Pistachio nuts contain lutein and zeaxanthin, which are protective antioxidants associated with eye health.

lemongrass frozen yogurt with basil

In Vietnamese cuisine, fresh herbs give the spicy rich food a remarkable lightness. Inspired by dishes where lemongrass delicately envelopes rich flavours, I came up with this recipe, which has become a personal favourite.

4 thin lemongrass stalks, washed and roughly chopped

180 ml / ¾ cup agave nectar

570 g / 2½ cups plain Greek yogurt (0% fat)

180 ml / ¾ cup organic low-fat milk

½ teaspoon finely grated lime zest

2 tablespoons freshly squeezed lime juice

2 tablespoons thinly shredded fresh purple Thai basil (or ordinary basil if unavailable)

an ice cream maker (optional)

Makes 1.4 litres / 1.5 quarts

Put the lemongrass and agave nectar in a small saucepan set over a medium/high heat. Bring to the boil and cook for 3–4 minutes, until the mixture becomes bubbly white. Remove from the heat and allow to sit for 5 further minutes so that the lemongrass taste infuses the agave nectar. Strain through a sieve to remove the lemongrass and set the nectar aside. Allow to cool completely.

Put the yogurt, milk, lime zest and lime juice in large bowl. Stir to combine. Pour in the lemongrass-scented agave nectar and add the basil. Stir well. Refrigerate the mixture until very cold.

Transfer to the bowl of an ice cream maker and churn according to the manufacturer's directions, until creamy and smooth. If you do not have an ice cream maker, pour the mixture into a freezerproof container. Put on the lid and place in the freezer. After about 45 minutes check the mixture. As it starts to freeze around the edges beat vigorously with a fork, whisk, electric hand mixer or spatula to break up the ice crystals. Repeat periodically until the mixture is frozen, about 2–3 hours. Serve in scoops.

♥ **lemongrass** (also known as citronella) has been widely used as a natural insect repellent. It has astringent, antimicrobial and antibacterial properties that stimulate digestion, regulate kidney function and help detoxify the liver. The essential oil in lemongrass contains myrcene, limonene and betacarotene, all beneficial for cell and tissue growth. It also has analgesic and calming qualities that help reduce pain and soothe skin irritations.

lemon lavender frozen yogurt

If you come across Meyer lemons, usually in season around January, do not hesitate to use them in this recipe. I just love the exquisite tangy yet floral taste of this delicious frozen yogurt.

720 ml / 3 cups plain Greek yogurt (0% fat)

2 tablespoons finely grated lemon zest

120 ml / ½ cup freshly squeezed lemon juice

180 ml / ¾ cup organic wild flower honey

1 tablespoon fresh lavender sprigs or ¼ teaspoon dried lavender

an ice cream maker (optional)

Makes 1.4 litres / 1.5 quarts

Put the yogurt, lemon zest and lemon juice in a large bowl and stir to combine.

Heat the honey and lavender in a small saucepan set over medium heat, until you can smell the lavender's scent. Strain through a fine sieve and allow to cool completely. Discard the lavender.

Add the lavender-infused honey to the yogurt and lemon juice mixture and stir to combine.

Transfer to the bowl of an ice cream maker and churn according to the manufacturer's directions, until creamy and smooth. If you do not have an ice cream maker, pour the mixture into a freezerproof container. Put on the lid and place in the freezer. After about 45 minutes check the mixture. As it starts to freeze around the edges beat vigorously with a fork, whisk, electric hand-held mixer or spatula to break up the ice crystals. Repeat periodically until the mixture is frozen, about 2–3 hours. Serve in small scoops.

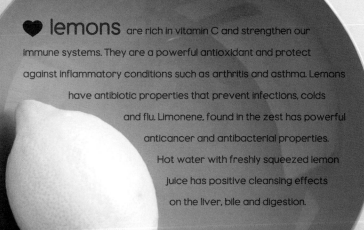

♥ **lemons** are rich in vitamin C and strengthen our immune systems. They are a powerful antioxidant and protect against inflammatory conditions such as arthritis and asthma. Lemons have antibiotic properties that prevent infections, colds and flu. Limonene, found in the zest has powerful anticancer and antibacterial properties. Hot water with freshly squeezed lemon juice has positive cleansing effects on the liver, bile and digestion.

chunky banana flax semifreddo

Semifreddos make great desserts for entertaining as they can be made in advance and simply removed from the freezer, turned out and sliced to serve.

3 egg yolks

400-ml / 13½-oz. can coconut milk

3 bananas, cut into chunks

120 ml / ½ cup agave nectar

2 tablespoons freshly squeezed lemon juice

25 g / ¼ cup chopped macadamia nuts

15 g / ½ oz. good-quality dark/bittersweet chocolate chunks

1 tablespoon ground linseed/flax seed meal

⅛ teaspoon sea salt

a 23 x 13 x 6-cm / 9 x 5 x-2½ inch loaf pan, fully lined with clingfilm/plastic wrap

Serves 6

Put the egg yolks and 120 ml / ½ cup of the coconut milk in a metal bowl set over a saucepan of gently simmering water. Whisk for 6 minutes, until the mixture has doubled in volume. Remove the bowl from the heat and continue whisking until cool.

Purée the bananas, agave nectar, lemon juice and remaining coconut milk in a blender until smooth. Stir into the egg and coconut mixture.

Pour half the mixture into the prepared loaf pan and smooth over the top. Cover loosely with clingfilm and put in the freezer for 1 hour. Store the remaining banana mixture in the refrigerator until required.

Remove the loaf pan from the freezer and sprinkle the macadamias, chocolate chunks and ground linseed/flax meal over the top. Pour in the remaining banana mixture, cover loosely with clingfilm and freeze for at least 4 hours. When ready to serve, turn out onto a platter, remove the clingfilm and slice.

 **bananas**

provide a good source of fructo-oligosaccharides, the preferred food for the 'friendly bacteria' that live in our digestive systems. They are also a good source of energy, rich in potassium and dietary fibre plus they prevent muscle cramps, help maintain a healthy heartbeat and regulate electrolyte and fluid balance.

bitter chocolate Earl Grey sorbet

Once, in a Manhattan tea house, I had a bitter chocolate biscuit dipped in Earl Grey tea. I never forgot how the strong flavours came together with such different qualities. This sorbet takes me back to that lovely afternoon of grown-up flavours.

180 ml / ¾ cup agave nectar

100 g / 1 cup good-quality cocoa powder

¼ teaspoon vanilla extract

¼ teaspoon sea salt

160 ml / ⅔ cup strong freshly brewed Earl Grey tea

Makes 1.4 litres / 1.5 quarts

Put the agave nectar, cocoa powder, vanilla, salt and tea in a large saucepan. Add 720 ml / 3 cups cold water and bring to the boil. Remove from the heat, and leave to cool completely in the refrigerator until very cold.

Transfer to the bowl of an ice cream maker and churn according to the manufacturer's directions. If you do not have an ice cream maker, pour the mixture into a freezerproof container. Put on the lid and place in the freezer. After 2 hours remove from the freezer and beat with an electric hand-held mixer to break down the frozen particles. Repeat periodically until the mixture is frozen. This will take about 2–3 hours.

Transfer the sorbet from the freezer to the refrigerator to soften about 10 minutes before serving. Serve in scoops.

♥ **black tea** contains potent polyphenols, powerful plant chemicals that protect our cells from oxidative stress. This anticancer activity repairs cellular damage and deactivates tumour growth. It is very effective in reducing the production of LDL 'bad' cholesterol and preventing cardiovascular disease.

almond coffee frozen yogurt sandwiches

This chilly treat is a wonderful 'caffeine quencher' afternoon snack on a hot day as well as being an impressive dessert for entertaining.

almond cookies

4 egg whites

275 g / 10 oz. flaked/slivered almonds

120 ml / ½ cup agave nectar

½ teaspoon vanilla extract

¼ teaspoon sea salt

coffee frozen yogurt

720 ml / 3 cups plain Greek yogurt (0% fat)

360 ml / 1½ cups organic fat-free milk

120 ml / ½ cup agave nectar

2 tablespoons Italian instant espresso powder

2 teaspoons freshly squeezed lemon juice

an ice cream maker (optional)

2 large baking sheets, greased and lined with parchment paper, also greased and dusted with flour

Makes 8

Preheat the oven to 160°C (325°F) Gas 3.

Put the egg whites, almonds, agave nectar, vanilla and salt in a bowl and stir until well combined. Use the back of a spoon to spread 2 tablespoons of the mixture on the prepared baking sheets in 8-cm / 3-inch rounds. Bake in the preheated oven for about 20–25 minutes, until the edges are golden brown.

Let the cookies cool for 10 minutes on the baking sheets then carefully lift them off and transfer to a wire rack to cool.

To make the coffee frozen yogurt, whisk together the yogurt, milk, agave nectar, espresso powder and lemon juice in a large bowl. Transfer to the bowl of an ice cream maker and churn according to the manufacturer's directions, until creamy and smooth. If you do not have an ice cream maker, pour the mixture into a freezerproof container. Put on the lid and place in the freezer. After about 45 minutes check the mixture. As it starts to freeze around the edges beat vigorously with a fork, whisk, electric hand mixer or spatula to break up the ice crystals. Repeat periodically until the mixture is frozen, about 2–3 hours.

To assemble the sandwiches, lay the cookies on a flat surface top. Spoon 2 tablespoons of coffee frozen yogurt onto half of the cookies. Top each one with the remaining cookies and press to make a sandwich. Transfer the sandwiches from the freezer to the refrigerator for at least 20 minutes before serving.

 coffee is a powerful stimulant containing chlorogenic acid and caffeic acid, both very strong antioxidants. When consumed in moderation coffee is surprisingly beneficial to health. It may help reduce the risk of heart disease and inflammatory conditions.

blackberry chocolate pops

Refreshing and indulgent, these are delicious and a big hit with the kids. I love the texture of the crunchy seeds as you bite into the frozen pop. If you like, you can replace the blackberries with raspberries or strawberries.

blackberry mixture

175 g / 6 oz. fresh blackberries

4 tablespoons agave nectar

1 teaspoon finely grated lemon zest

2 tablespoons freshly squeezed lemon juice

chocolate mixture

4 tablespoons agave nectar

25 g / ⅓ cup good-quality cocoa powder

1 teaspoon vanilla extract

an 8 x 75-g / 3-oz. capacity ice lolly/popsicle mould or similar

8 wooden sticks

Makes 8

Put the blackberries, agave nectar, lemon zest and lemon juice in the bowl of a food processor or a blender. Add 180 ml / ¾ cup cold water and purée until smooth.

Pour the blackberry mixture into the moulds, filling each one just half way. Freeze for up to 1 hour.

In the meantime prepare the chocolate mixture. Put the agave nectar, cocoa and vanilla in a small saucepan set over medium heat. Add 180 ml / ¾ cup cold water and bring to the boil, whisking continuously until the cocoa dissolves completely. Remove from the heat, let cool then chill thoroughly.

Remove the pops from the freezer and spoon the chocolate mixture into the moulds, on top of the blackberry mixture. Return to the freezer. After 30 minutes remove the pops from the freezer and insert a wooden stick in the centre of each one. Return to the freezer and freeze until completely frozen and firm before serving.

♥ **blackberries** are loaded with potent antioxidants. They contain polyphenols that help lower the risk of heart disease and protect against cancer. Anthocyanins, which give these berries their dark colour, reduce inflammation. They contain ellagic acid which protects the skin from UV rays, restores skin cells and repairs sun damage. Blackberries are also rich in vitamin C, manganese and dietary fibre.

honeydew melon granita

Smelling the rind of honeydew melons in search of ripeness is a pleasure in itself. Sweet, earthy and floral aromas will come through when you have found the perfect melon to enjoy. I love making this granita at the peak of summer!

450 g / 1 lb. honeydew melon chunks (a 1.5-kg / 3.5-lb. melon)

¼ teaspoon chopped jalapeño pepper

60 ml / ¼ cup agave nectar

2 tablespoons freshly squeezed lime juice

a 20-cm / 8-inch square metal baking pan

Makes about 1 litre / quart

Put the melon, jalapeño pepper, agave nectar and lime juice in the bowl of a food processor or blender and add 120 ml / ½ cup cold water. Purée until completely blended.

Pour the melon mixture into the pan and freeze for 4 hours. Remove from the freezer and using a fork, scrape the surface with a fork until flakes form.

Cover loosely with clingfilm/plastic wrap and return to the freezer. Keep frozen until ready to serve.

❤ **honeydew melons** are a high-volume, low-calorie food that is ideal for weight loss as they supply mostly water and fibre. They are a good source of potassium, which is a key component for a healthy heart and blood pressure levels. Honeydew melons also contain vitamins C and A which strengthen our immune systems and help our skin.

guava freeze

These creamy ice cubes are both unexpected and fun. The musky guava and satiny vanilla are a delightful marriage of flavours.

720 ml / 3 cups guava juice

40 ml / 2 cups low-fat vanilla-flavoured yogurt

125 ml / ½ cup agave nectar

1 tablespoon freshly squeezed lime juice

¼ teaspoon sea salt

1 teaspoon finely grated lime zest, to decorate

ice cube trays (square or shaped as preferred)

Serves 6 (makes about 30 cubes)

Put the guava juice, yogurt, agave nectar, lime juice and salt in a medium bowl and stir until well combined. Pour the mixture into ice cube trays and freeze for 4 hours or until firm.

Divide the ice cubes among 6 serving bowls and decorate with grated lime zest. Serve immediately.

♥ **guavas** are considered one of the most nutritious foods available to us. They contain the highest concentration of lycopene present in any fruit or vegetable. This is a potent antioxidant that helps prevents cancer and repair damaged cells. They are very rich in potassium, magnesium and vitamins C and A. Guavas are also an excellent source of dietary fibre.

toppings

(to be enjoyed with your own home-made frozen yogurt or with Snog frozen yogurt)

peanut pineapple chunks

Any excuse to eat sweet and caramelized pineapple is a good excuse. The peanut butter here adds the creamy nutty coating that keeps you craving more.

450 g / 1 lb. fresh pineapple, cubed

70 g / ¼ cup smooth organic peanut butter

60 ml / ¼ cup agave nectar

60 ml / ¼ cup canned tamarind juice

2 tablespoons peanut oil

Snog Pure Frozen Yogurt (see page 20), to serve

a baking sheet, lightly greased

Serves 8

Preheat the oven to 190°C (375°F) Gas 5.

Put the pineapple, peanut butter, agave nectar, tamarind juice and oil in a large bowl and mix well to combine and coat the pineapple chunks.

Spread the chunks out onto the prepared baking sheet and bake in the preheated oven for 12–15 minutes, until the edges of the pineapple become dark and crispy and the juices have thickened.

Remove from the oven and allow to cool. Spoon over scoops of your favourite Snog Pure Frozen Yogurt to serve.

The peanut pineapple chunks can be stored in an airtight container in the refrigerator for up to 3 days.

💙 **peanuts** are not really nuts. They are actually legumes that grow as a ground flower, burrow into the earth and mature underground. They are high in antioxidant power and contain cancer-fighting p-coumaric acid. Peanuts are a good source of niacin, folic acid, copper, vitamin E, protein and manganese, and are rich in monounsaturated fat which helps promotes good heart health.

candied rhubarb with strawberries and basil

Here the tangy sweet fruit and fresh basil come together in a delicate and aromatic combination. The rhubarb is marinated overnight so you'll need to plan ahead.

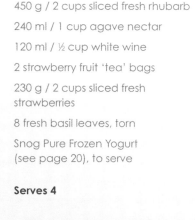

450 g / 2 cups sliced fresh rhubarb

240 ml / 1 cup agave nectar

120 ml / ½ cup white wine

2 strawberry fruit 'tea' bags

230 g / 2 cups sliced fresh strawberries

8 fresh basil leaves, torn

Snog Pure Frozen Yogurt
(see page 20), to serve

Serves 4

Put the rhubarb in a heat-resistant bowl. Put the wine and agave nectar in a saucepan set over medium heat and add 240 ml / 1 cup cold water. Bring to the boil and add the strawberry 'tea' bags. Cover and remove from the heat. Let stand for 5 minutes.

Remove the 'tea' bags, bring the liquid back to the boil and then carefully pour it over the sliced rhubarb. Cover tightly with clingfilm/plastic wrap and allow to cool completely. Refrigerate overnight and stir in the strawberries and basil leaves just before serving. Spoon over scoops of your favourite Snog Pure Frozen Yogurt to serve. This topping is best enjoyed on the day it is made.

♥ rhubarb is very rich in calcium and oxalic acid. It is a very good source of dietary fibre and aids indigestion. Fresh rhubarb has antibacterial and anti-inflammatory properties that help lower the risk of high blood pressure and maintain healthy levels of cholesterol. Rhubarb is also used in Chinese medicine to cure constipation.

blueberry ginger-lemon sauce

A fragrant sauce that calls to mind the summery scent of fresh berries and the soothing qualities of ginger.

400 g / 2 pints fresh blueberries

1 tablespoon finely grated
lemon zest

60 ml / ¼ cup freshly squeezed
lemon juice

3 tablespoons agave nectar

2 tablespoons finely grated
fresh ginger

Snog Pure Frozen Yogurt
(see page 20), to serve

Serves 8

Put the blueberries, lemon zest, lemon juice, agave nectar and ginger in the bowl of a food processor or a blender and purée until very smooth. Spoon over scoops of your favourite Snog Pure Frozen Yogurt to serve.

The sauce can be stored in an airtight container in the refrigerator for up to 3 days.

dried ginger black and white sesame crisps

A classic dessert enjoyed in the Middle East is fresh yogurt served with honey and toasted sesame seeds. It's a beautifully balanced combination that, with the addition of cashews and ginger, becomes a scrumptious complement to Snog's Green Tea Frozen Yogurt or the crisps can be enjoyed on their own.

50 g / ½ cup chopped roasted cashew nuts

3 tablespoons toasted white sesame seeds

3 tablespoons black sesame seeds

120 ml / ½ cup agave nectar

2 tablespoons desiccated ginger

1 egg white

25 g / ¼ cup coconut flour

¼ teaspoon sea salt

Snog Green Tea Pure Frozen Yogurt (see page 20), to serve (optional)

a baking sheet, lined with baking parchment

Makes 18–20

Preheat the oven to 160°C (325°F) Gas 3.

Lightly whisk the egg white in a large bowl. Add the cashews, white and black sesame seeds, agave nectar, ginger, coconut flour and salt. Stir to combine completely, until all the ingredients come together in a sticky mixture.

Place heaped teaspoonfuls of the mixture on the prepared baking sheet. Flatten to create 5-cm / 2-inch rounds.

Bake in the preheated oven for 25–30 minutes, until golden and crisp. Allow to cool completely. Serve with generous scoops of Snog Green Tea Pure Frozen Yogurt.

Once cold, these crisps will keep stored in an airtight container for up to 5 days.

♥ **sesame seeds** have been valued since ancient times for their nutty flavour and oil. They are a good source of protein and rich in copper, manganese, iron, magnesium and calcium. Sesame seeds contain lingans, a group of beneficial fibres that include sesamin and sesaminol. These enhance the absorption of vitamin E and increase the activity of liver enzymes that help break down fat.

roasted summer fruits

Make sure all the fruit you are using is ripe and sweet; nothing is worse than a mealy nectarine or peach. Adding a little wine is a sort of welcome to the upcoming grape harvest but feel free to replace with unsweetened grape juice, if preferred.

1 large peach, cut into 5-mm / ¼-inch wedges

1 large nectarine, cut into 5-mm / ¼-inch wedges

1 ripe plum, cut into 5-mm / ¼-inch wedges

8 sweet fresh cherries, pitted and halved

4 tablespoons agave nectar

¼ teaspoon freshly ground black pepper

4 tablespoons red wine or 4 tablespoons unsweetened grape juice

Snog Natural Pure Frozen Yogurt (see page 20), to serve

a rimmed baking sheet, lined with parchment paper

Serves 4–6

Preheat the oven to 180°C (350°F) Gas 4.

Put the peach, nectarine and plum slices and the cherries onto the prepared baking sheet.

Put the agave nectar, black pepper and red wine in a small bowl and whisk until combined. Drizzle over the fruit and bake in the preheated oven for 25–30 minutes, until golden, juicy and partially caramelized. Allow the roasted fruit to cool slightly on the baking sheet.

Serve warm, spooned over generous scoops of Snog Natural Pure Frozen Yogurt.

These roasted fruits will keep stored in an airtight container in the refrigerator for up to 3 days.

♥ **cherries** have anti-inflammatory properties and are potent cancer-fighting agents. They are a good source of potassium and vitamin A. Cherries contain quercetin and ellagic acid, which fight cancer cells and inhibit tumour growth. They also have antiviral and antibacterial properties.

dark chocolate and cashew slivers

This summery mixture of dried fruits and nuts works beautifully but you can try any combination you like, such as dried pineapple and pistachios or raisins and almonds. Although the cacao nibs are optional they do add a wonderful crunch to every bite.

225 g / 8 oz. good-quality dark/bittersweet chocolate (70% cocoa solids), chopped

2 teaspoons agave nectar

60 g / ½ cup roasted cashew nuts

45 g / ¼ cup dried blueberries

45 g / ¼ cup dried nectarines, chopped

1 tablespoon cacao nibs (optional)

Snog Pure Frozen Yogurt (see page 20), to serve

a baking sheet, lined with parchment paper

Serves 8

Put the chocolate in a heat-resistant bowl set over a saucepan of gently simmering water. Do not let the base of the bowl touch the water. Stir continuously until melted.

Remove from the heat and stir in the agave nectar. Pour onto the prepared baking sheet. Spread out using the back of a metal spoon or a metal spatula and sprinkle liberally with the cashews, dried fruit and cacao nibs.

Allow to cool on the baking sheet at room temperature for 2–3 hours, until hard. Break into large shards and serve with generous scoops of your favourite Snog Pure Frozen Yogurt.

These slivers will keep stored in an airtight container in a cool place for up to 3 days.

♥ **cacao nibs** are bursting with vitamins, minerals, antioxidants and theobromine – a chemical that makes you feel good. It is also a rich food source of chromium, which helps maintain balanced blood sugar levels. Cacao contains magnesium, which assists the body in most of its functions. The flavonols in raw cacao contain one of the best sources of antioxidant protection available.

pomegranate, white chocolate and peppermint mix

Pomegranate seeds could be described as tangy sweet jewels. The subtle taste of white chocolate and the intense aroma of natural peppermint contrast with the seeds here to create a combination sublime in both texture and taste.

120 g / 1 cup toasted walnuts, roughly chopped

100 g / ½ cup good-quality white chocolate chunks

2 tablespoons small fresh peppermint leaves

80 g / ½ cup pomegranate seeds

1 tablespoon pomegranate molasses

Snog Pure Frozen Yogurt (see page 20), to serve

Serves 6–8

Combine the walnuts, chocolate chunks, peppermint leaves and pomegranate seeds in a small bowl. Add the pomegranate molasses and stir well to coat all of the ingredients.

Serve sprinkled over generous scoops of your favourite Snog Pure Frozen Yogurt.

This topping will keep stored in an airtight container in the refrigerator for 2–3 days.

♥ **peppermint** helps relax the smooth muscle that surrounds the intestine. This relieves indigestion and prevents colonic muscle spasms. Peppermint oil has anticancer, antibacterial and antifungal properties. It contains rosmarinic acid, a substance that helps respiratory conditions such as asthma and allergic rhinitis. Peppermint is a good source of manganese and vitamins C and A.

crushed dates and figs with cherries and spice

Allspice is a complex ingredient, it tastes like cinnamon, nutmeg and cloves blended together but it is in fact a kind of berry that once dried has this unique aroma. The flavours of dates, dried cherries and orange gives this topping a wintery feel.

80 g / ½ cup sliced pitted Medjool dates

80 g / ½ cup chopped dried figs

40 g / ¼ cup sour cherries

⅛ teaspoon ground allspice

2 teaspoons agave nectar

1 tablespoon coconut or almond oil

1 tablespoon freshly squeezed orange juice

Snog Chocolate Pure Frozen Yogurt (see page 20), to serve

Serves 4

Combine the dates, figs, cherries, allspice, agave nectar, coconut oil and orange juice in a large bowl. Let stand at room temperature for at least 10 minutes, to allow the flavours to mingle.

Serve spooned over generous scoops of Snog Chocolate Pure Frozen Yogurt.

These fruits will keep stored in an airtight container in the refrigerator for up to 3 days.

♥ figs are a good source of instant sugar that stimulates our brain and lowers high blood pressure. They are low in fat and very high in fibre, which can assist weight loss. Figs make a healthy snack as they are packed with calcium, iron, magnesium and potassium. They also contain trytophan and can help promote a healthy good night's sleep.

slivered pears with fennel and lemony drizzle

Sweet pears combined with the crisp liquorice taste of fennel are a delightful treat, especially when paired with natural frozen yogurt. The texture of the fennel should be chewy, in contrast with the softened pears.

1 fennel bulb, trimmed and very thinly sliced

160 ml / ⅔ cup agave nectar

1 tablespoon finely grated lemon zest

3 tablespoons freshly squeezed lemon juice

⅛ teaspoon sea salt

2 Anjou, Conference or Comice pears, peeled, cored and thinly sliced

Snog Natural Pure Frozen Yogurt (see page 20), to serve

Serves 4

Put the fennel, agave nectar, lemon zest, lemon juice and salt in a large saucepan and set over medium heat.

Add 240 ml / 1 cup cold water and bring to a simmer. Cook for about 10 minutes, until the fennel begins to turn translucent.

Add the sliced pears to the pan and cook for a further 10–15 minutes, until the pears are tender but still hold their shape.

Transfer to a plastic container and allow to cool in the refrigerator until ready to use. Spoon, along with any juices, over Snog Natural Pure Frozen Yogurt to serve.

This topping will keep stored in an airtight container in the refrigerator for up to 2 days.

♥ **fennel** provides potent antioxidant protection. It is a rich source of vitamin C, which is antimicrobial and protects the immune system. Fennel contains dietary fibre, folate and potassium. It lowers the levels of LDL 'bad' cholesterol and helps reduce the risk of heart disease. Fennel also relieves abdominal gas and helps with cramps.

cinnamon sweet potatoes with salty pumpkin seeds

Sweet and salty flavours are marvellous when enjoyed together. This unusual topping beautifully enhances the tangy taste of Snog frozen yogurt.

1 sweet potato (about 280 g / 10 oz.) cut into 5-mm / ¼-inch dice

2 tablespoons roasted salted hulled pumpkin seeds (see note)

2 tablespoons sultanas/golden raisins

¼ teaspoon ground cinnamon

1 tablespoon palm/date sugar or 2 teaspoons agave nectar

2 teaspoons coconut oil

Snog Pure Frozen Yogurt (see page 20), to serve

Serves 4–6

Preheat the oven to 190°C (375°F) Gas 5

Put the sweet potatoes, pumpkin seeds and sultanas on a baking sheet. Sprinkle over the cinnamon and palm sugar or agave nectar, drizzle with the coconut oil and stir to coat all the ingredients.

Bake in the preheated oven for 25 minutes, stirring 2 or 3 times, until evenly roasted and the sweet potatoes are tender and starting to caramelize.

Let cool on the baking sheet for 5 minutes. Serve sprinkled over generous scoops your favourite Snog Pure Frozen Yogurt.

This topping will keep stored in an airtight container in the refrigerator for up to 2 days.

Note: If you cannot find roasted salted hulled pumpkin seeds, you can make them by tossing some hulled pumpkin seeds lightly in olive oil then put on a baking sheet and sprinkle with sea salt. Bake in an oven preheated to 150°C (300°F) Gas 2 for about 30–40 minutes, stirring every 10 minutes, until roasted.

♥ **sweet potatoes** are not really a potato – they are the healthiest starchy root vegetable available and belong to the morning glory family. They are loaded with fibre, primarily in the skin and are a rich source of betacarotene, vitamins A and C, manganese, potassium and iron.

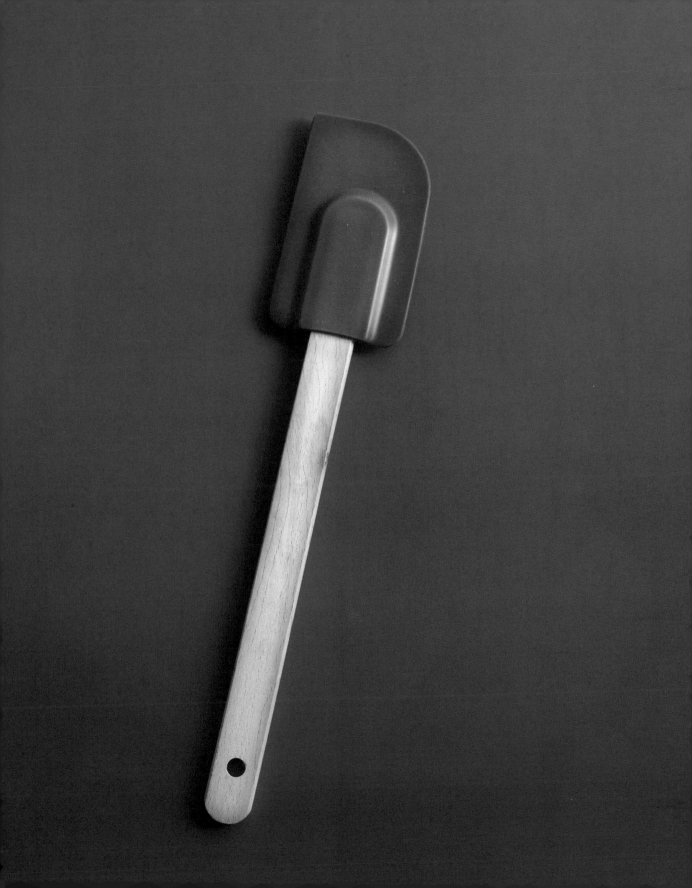

gluten-free
baked treats

Snog chocolate 'brownies'

This delicious brownie-style slice is not only gluten-free but the recipe has no added sugar either (though the chocolate you use may contain a small amount) so it's an indulgent treat without the guilt! Serve them just-baked and warm from the oven.

250 g / 9 oz. good-quality dark/bittersweet chocolate (85% cocoa solids), broken into chunks

175 g / 1½ sticks unsalted butter, cubed

3 eggs

150 ml / ⅔ cup agave nectar

1 teaspoon vanilla extract

75 g / ¼ cup ground almonds/almond meal

100 g / 1 scant cup gluten-free plain/all-purpose flour (such as Doves Farm or Bob's Red Mill)

16 walnut halves

plain Greek yogurt (0% fat), to serve (optional)

a 25-cm / 10-inch square baking pan, lightly greased and base-lined with parchment paper

Makes 16

Preheat the oven to 180°C (350°F) Gas 4.

Put the chocolate and butter in a heat-resistant bowl set over a saucepan of barely simmering water. (Do not let the base of the bowl touch the water.) Stir continuously until melted and combined then remove from the heat and let cool slightly.

Put the eggs, agave nectar and vanilla in a large bowl and whisk together. Pour in the melted chocolate and butter and mix together until smooth.

Stir in the ground almonds and flour until combined. Spoon the mixture in the prepared baking pan and level the surface with a spatula. Top with the walnut halves and bake in the preheated oven for 12–15 minutes, until just set.

Leave to cool slightly in the pan before cutting into squares. Serve warm with a dollop of Greek-style yogurt on the side, if liked.

Once cold, these brownies will keep stored in an airtight container for up to 5 days. They can be wrapped in foil and gently reheated in a low oven if you wish to serve them warm.

Oaxacan brownie bites with almond chocolate sauce

The Mayans had it right: chocolate and spice. Their culture, in which balance of energy and alignment of the planets and stars were the core, has taught us that combining what seem to be extreme flavours really works. I love this treat because it satisfies a chocolate craving and also gives a kick of spice!

50 g / ¼ cup chickpea flour

25 g / ⅛ cup brown rice flour

25 g / ⅛ cup potato flour

25 g / ⅛ cup cocoa powder

1 teaspoon baking powder

⅛ teaspoon bicarbonate of soda/baking soda

⅛ teaspoon xantham gum

½ teaspoon sea salt

½ teaspoon chilli powder (ideally smoked, such as chipotle)

120 ml / ½ cup grapeseed oil

60 ml / ¼ cup agave nectar

60 ml / ¼ cup apple sauce

1½ teaspoons vanilla extract

60 ml / ¼ cup hot water

chocolate almond sauce

50 g / 2 oz. good-quality dark/bittersweet chocolate (70% cocoa solids), broken into chunks

1 tablespoon almond butter

1 tablespoon agave nectar

a 12-hole mini cupcake pan, lightly oiled

Makes 12

Preheat the oven to 160°C (325°F) Gas 3.

Sift the flours, cocoa powder, baking powder, baking soda, xantham gum, salt and chilli powder into a large bowl and stir to combine.

In a separate bowl, combine the grapeseed oil, agave nectar, apple sauce and vanilla. Pour this mixture into the flour mixture and stir with a spatula until just incorporated. Pour in the hot water and stir until combined. Do not overmix.

Spoon the mixture into the prepared baking pan. Bake in the preheated oven for 20–25 minutes, until the surface of the brownies are crisp and a skewer inserted in the centre comes out just clean. Let cool in the pan.

To make the chocolate almond sauce, put the chocolate in a heat-resistant bowl set over a pan of barely simmerling water. (Do not let the base of the bowl touch the water.) Stir continuously until melted. Remove from the heat and let cool before stirring in the almond butter and agave nectar. Spoon a little of the sauce on top of each brownie bite to serve.

♥ **cocoa powder** is loaded with compounds called flavonols. These protect us from environmental toxins and prevent the fats in our blood from clotting. They support heart health and regulate blood circulation. Cocoa is rich in magnesium, iron, phosphorous, copper and potassium and also a good source of protein and dietary fibre.

tangerine olive oil hazelnut cake

Inspired by an Italian classic, this olive oil cake is moist and citrusy. The earthy taste of the hazelnuts makes this an ideal accompaniment to a cup of hot coffee or tea.

125 g / 1 cup plain/
all-purpose gluten-free
flour (such as Doves Farm
or Bob's Red Mill)*

25 g / ¼ cup brown rice
flour

75 g / 3 oz. toasted
hazelnuts

1½ teaspoons baking
powder

1 teaspoon bicarbonate
of soda/baking soda

½ teaspoon sea salt

1 teaspoon xantham gum

2 eggs

200 ml / ¾ cup agave
nectar

50 ml / ⅓ cup buttermilk

100 ml / ½ scant cup extra
virgin olive oil

1 tablespoon finely grated
tangerine zest

*a 23-cm / 9-inch cake
pan, greased and lined*

Serves 8–10

Preheat the oven to 160°C (325°F) Gas 3.

Put the flours, hazelnuts, baking powder, bicarbonate of soda and salt in a food processor. Pulse a few times until the hazelnuts are finely ground. Transfer to a large bowl and stir in the xantham gum.

In a separate bowl, whisk together the eggs, agave nectar, buttermilk, olive oil and zest until combined. Pour this mixture into the flour mixture and fold in until the ingredients are well incorporated but do not overmix.

Pour the mixture into the prepared tin/pan and bake in the preheated oven for 40–45 minutes, until the cake rises and springs back to the touch. Let cool in the tin/pan on a wire rack for 10 minutes and then turn out the cake to cool completely.

Cut into slices and serve with a scoop of Snog's Natural Pure Frozen Yogurt (see page 20) or a dollop of Greek-style yogurt.

Note As brands of gluten-free flour can vary, we recommend adding liquid ingredients a little at a time, until the batter is of a very thick pouring consistency.

❤ **olive oil** has high levels of phenols, strong antioxidant compounds. Its main component oleic acid is a monounsaturated fat. This is a heart-healthy fat. Olive oil is beneficial in reducing LDL 'bad' cholesterol levels and lowering high blood pressure. It contains vitamin E and provides excellent nourishment to the skin, nails and hair.

chocolate avocado cream pie

Avocados and chocolate are both decadent and surprising together. The gloss and smooth texture of the mousse here is startling, a perfect balance between two tropical ingredients. Make sure to wrap the pie very well with clingfilm if not consuming right away – though this is unlikely!

pie crust

100 g / 1 cup macadamia nuts, plus 2 tablespoons to decorate

100 g / ¾ cup brown rice flour

2 tablespoons palm/date sugar or light soft brown sugar

¼ teaspoon baking powder

¼ teaspoon sea salt

3 tablespoons grapeseed oil

4 tablespoons agave nectar

filling

2 large ripe avocados, peeled and pitted

120 ml / ½ cup agave nectar

2 teaspoons vanilla extract

120 ml / ½ cup coconut milk

75 g / ¾ cup good-quality cocoa powder

1 tablespoon coconut oil or grapeseed oil

½ teaspoon sea salt

a 30 x 10 cm / 12 x 4 inch tart pan

Serves 8

To make the pie crust, put 100 g / 1 cup of the macadamias in the bowl of a food processor or a blender and process to a fine meal. Transfer to a mixing bowl.

Add the rice flour, palm or brown sugar, baking powder and salt to the ground macadamias. Mix until all the ingredients are well combined.

Put the oil and agave nectar in a small bowl and mix to combine. Pour this into the macadamia mixture and stir thoroughly until well incorporated. Spoon the mixture into the tart pan. Using the tips of damp fingers, press to distribute evenly

on the bottom and sides of the pan. Freeze for 25 minutes.

Preheat the oven to 180°C (350°F) Gas 4. Bake the chilled pie crust in the preheated oven for about 15 minutes, until golden. Let cool completely in the pan.

To make the mousse filling, put the avocados, agave nectar, vanilla, coconut milk, cocoa powder, coconut oil and salt in the bowl of a food processor. Purée until smooth.

Spread the filling evenly on the chilled tart crust and garnish with the remaining chopped macadamias. Serve cut into slices.

If not eating right away, wrap very tightly in clingfilm/plastic wrap and refrigerate for up to 3–4 hours.

This pie is best enjoyed on the day it is made.

♥ macadamia nuts

are really good for you. They contain the highest level of monounsaturated fat available. This is very healthy oil that helps reduce the risk of heart disease and lower LDL 'bad' cholesterol levels. These nuts contain calcium, phosphorous, potassium, magnesium and selenium. They are associated with longevity and promote good prostate health.

peach tartlets with maple cream

Three is a crowd but not when it comes to putting together maple, almond and summer ripe peaches. I adore this combination because not only can you taste each individual flavour but the contrast between the crunchy crust and the smooth filling is delicious. The peaches can be replaced with nectarines or plums if liked.

50 g / ¾ cup toasted flaked/slivered almonds

100 g / ¾ cup plain/all-purpose gluten-free flour (such as Doves Farm or Bob's Red Mill)

1 tablespoon plus 1 teaspoon coconut oil

60 ml / ¼ cup agave nectar

100 g / 4 oz. cream cheese

3 tablespoons maple syrup

2 tablespoons almond milk

¼ teaspoon vanilla extract

3 small ripe peaches, pitted and cut into eighths

6 x 12-cm / 4½-inch diameter, loose-based fluted tartlet pans

Serves 6

To make the tartlet crust, put the almonds, flour, coconut oil and agave nectar in the bowl of a food processor and pulse until coarsely ground. The mixture will come together into a paste.

Transfer to the tartlet pans and using the tips of damp fingers press to distribute evenly on the bottom and sides of the pans. Freeze for 30 minutes.

Preheat the oven to 180°C (350°F) Gas 4. Bake the chilled tartlet crusts in the preheated oven for about 15 minutes, until golden. Allow to cool completely in the pans and set on a wire rack.

To make the filling, put the cream cheese, maple syrup, almond milk and vanilla in a mixing bowl and using a hand-held electric mixer, beat until light and airy. Spoon the mixture into the cooled tartlet crusts and level the surfaces with a palette knife. Arrange 4 peach slices on top of each tartlet and refrigerate until ready to serve.

These tartlets are best enjoyed on the day they are made.

♥ **peaches** are a delicious treat with moderate calories. They are rich in phytonutrients and rank high in anti-inflammatory and antioxidant activity. They contain calcium, magnesium, phosphorous, potassium and vitamins A, C and K. Peaches help us maintain healthy skin and add colour to our complexions.

coconut apricot macaroons

This is a classic gluten-free recipe but you can replace the apricots with any dried fruit you like: cherries, pineapples, mangoes, you name it – they all work beautifully. I recommend you use very good quality dark chocolate for the best results.

3 egg whites

175 g / 2½ cups sweetened shredded dried coconut

5 tablespoons agave nectar

50 g / ¼ cup chopped dried apricots

25 g / 1 oz. good-quality dark/bittersweet chocolate, melted

a baking sheet, lined with parchment paper

Makes 18

Preheat the oven to 150°C (300°F) Gas 2.

Put the egg whites in a spotlessly clean metal or glass bowl and whisk until light and frothy.

Add the coconut, agave nectar and apricots and stir just to combine. Form teaspoon-size cookies using your hands to shape into mounds, and place on the prepared baking sheet.

Bake in the preheated oven for 12–14 minutes, until golden around the edges and on the top. Let cool on the baking sheet.

When the macaroons are completely cool, drizzle over the melted chocolate and let set before serving. The macaroons will keep for up to 4 days if stored in an airtight container.

♥ **egg whites** are one of the best sources of low-fat, high-quality protein available. They are cholesterol free and provide sodium, potassium, selenium and vitamin B. They are a low-calorie food with negligible carbohydrates so ideal for anyone following a weight-loss program.

icebox chestnut fennel cookies

Icebox cookies are a childhood treat. Adding currants and fennel gives this classically simple biscuit a sophisticated spin. These cookies are ideal for accompanying a cup of fruit tea or a glass of Vin Santo.

50 g / ¼ cup chestnut flour

200 g / 2 cups plain/all-purpose gluten-free flour (such as Doves Farm or Bob's Red Mill)

½ teaspoon toasted fennel seeds

½ teaspoon sea salt

225 g / 2 sticks unsalted butter, softened

3 tablespoons agave nectar

1 egg

1 teaspoon vanilla extract

50 g / ¼ cup currants

a baking sheet, lined with parchment paper

Makes 24

Preheat the oven to 160°C (325°F) Gas 3.

Put the chestnut flour, gluten-free flour, fennel seeds and salt in a mixing bowl and stir to combine.

Put the butter in a metal or glass bowl and using a hand-held electric mixer, beat until light and airy. Add the agave nectar and whisk into the butter. Add the egg and vanilla and continue whisking until incorporated.

Add the flour mixture to the butter mixture, alternating with the currants. Fold in using a rubber spatula until the dough comes together, do not overmix. Transfer the cookie dough to a lightly floured surface and form into 2 logs. Wrap with clingfilm/plastic wrap and freeze for at least 1 hour.

Before baking, cut the logs into ½-cm / ¼-inch thick rounds. Put the rounds on the prepared baking sheet, spacing them about 2.5 cm / 1 inch apart. Bake in the preheated oven for about 12–15 minutes, until golden.

Leave to cool on the baking sheet for 5 minutes before transferring to a wire rack to cool completely. The cookies will keep for up to 5 days if stored in an airtight container.

❤ **chestnuts** are low in both fat and calories, and have a high starch content. They are rich in copper, magnesium, manganese and vitamin C. They are beneficial in reducing LDL 'bad' cholesterol levels and regulating blood pressure. Chestnuts are rich in dietary fibre and can help us lose weight when eaten in moderation.

oaty cookies

A comforting treat, gluten-free style – this large chewy cookie is delicious with a cup of hot coffee. The scent coming from your oven while these bake makes this recipe well worth it before you've even taken a bite!

113 g / 1 stick butter, softened

360 ml / 1½ cups agave nectar

3 eggs

75 g / ½ cup rice flour

75 g / ½ cup plain/all-purpose gluten-free flour (such as Doves Farm or Bob's Red Mill)

1 teaspoon xantham gum

1½ teaspoons bicarbonate of soda/baking soda

½ teaspoon cinnamon

40 g / ¼ cup raisins

130 g / 1½ cups gluten-free rolled oats

2 baking sheets, lined with parchment paper

Makes 12

Preheat the oven to 180°C (350°F) Gas 4.

Put the butter and agave nectar in a food mixer with a paddle attachment and cream until light and fluffy. Add the eggs, one at a time, mixing after each addition. Scrape the sides of the bowl with a rubber spatula to incorporate any unmixed ingredients. (Alternatively, use a large bowl and a hand-held electric mixer.)

Add the flours, xantham gum, bicarbonate of soda, cinnamon, raisins and oats and mix well, but do not overmix.

Place tablespoons of the mixture on the prepared baking sheets, spaced about 2.5 cm / ½ inch.

Bake in the preheated oven for 10–12 minutes, until lightly golden. Let the cookies cool for 5 minutes on the baking sheets before carefully transferring to a wire rack to cool completely. These cookies will keep for up to 5 days if stored in an airtight container.

♥ **oats** are one of the most nutritious grains. They are high in soluble fibre and also contain vitamin E and some B vitamins, as well as iron and calcium. They contain beta-glucans that enhance the immune system, significantly lower the levels of LDL 'bad' cholesterol, and help reduce the risk of heart disease. Oats are also rich in avenathramide, a potent antioxidant with anti-inflammatory properties.

mini blueberry scones

When it comes to treats I'm convinced that not only is the quality of the ingredients important, but also the amount you eat. I came up with this recipe when thinking up a sweet bite for the morning time that is good for you but also a sensible size. Plus, who doesn't want blueberry scones for breakfast?

130 g / 1 cup chickpea flour

1 teaspoon baking powder

¼ teaspoon sea salt

¼ teaspoon ground cinnamon

⅛ teaspoon ground allspice

25 g / 2 tablespoons cold unsalted butter, cut into small dice

1 egg

3 tablespoons milk, plus a little extra to glaze

60 ml / ¼ cup agave nectar

40 g / ¼ cup fresh blueberries

a baking sheet, lightly greased

Makes 12

Preheat the oven to 180°C (350°F) Gas 4.

Sift together the flour, baking powder, salt, cinnamon and allspice into a large bowl. Add the butter and work with your hands until the mixture resembles crumbly sand.

Add the egg, milk and the agave nectar and continue working the dough, without overmixing, until it starts to come together. The mixture will be very sticky.

Add the blueberries and mix in very gently with your hands. Lightly flour the work surface and your hands to prevent the mixture from sticking. Shape the dough into a single piece, 7.5 x 10 cm / 3 x 4 inches in size and 1 cm / ½ inch thick.

Using a sharp serrated knife, cut the dough into 2.5-cm / 1-inch squares and put these on the prepared baking sheet. Brush lightly with milk to glaze and bake in the preheated oven for 12–14 minutes, until golden. Serve warm.

Once cool, these scones will keep for 2–3 days if stored in an airtight container.

passion fruit orange blossom custard cake

Coconut flour is something I came across only recently in this journey discovering gluten-free foods. The surprise is that it doesn't feel like a substitute but an enriching ingredient that makes the texture interesting and works as a binder. This recipe is adapted from my aunt's orange blossom custard cakes.

2 eggs, separated

180 ml / ¾ cup fat-free buttermilk

60 ml / ¼ cup natural passion fruit juice

½ teaspoon finely grated orange zest

½ teaspoon orange-flower water

¼ teaspoon sea salt

2 tablespoons coconut flour

25 g / ¼ cup chopped toasted pistachios

4 individual ramekins or custard cups, lightly oiled

a deep-sided roasting pan, large enough to take the ramekins

Serves 4

Preheat the oven to 160°C (325°F) Gas 3.

Put the egg yolks, buttermilk, passion fruit juice, orange zest, orange-flower water, salt and coconut flour in a mixing bowl and beat until combined.

Put the egg whites in a spotlessly clean bowl and using a hand-held electric mixer, whisk on medium speed until frothy. Increase the speed as the whites become foamier. Whisk until soft peaks form.

Fold the egg whites into the passion fruit mixture until combined. Spoon into the prepared ramekins and transfer to the roasting pan. Transfer to the preheated oven and carefully add enough water to come halfway up the sides of the ramekins. Bake for 20–25 minutes, until the filling is no longer wobbly and the tops are slightly golden.

Remove the ramekins from the water bath and allow to cool slightly on a wire rack. To serve, either leave in the ramekins or run a knife around the edge of the ramekins and turn the cakes out onto serving plates. Sprinkle each one with chopped pistachios and serve. Alternatively, cover with clingfilm/plastic wrap and transfer to the refrigerator to chill until ready to serve. These cakes are best enjoyed on the day they are made.

❤ **passion fruit** is a good source of potassium and vitamins A and C. Its seeds are an excellent source of dietary fibre. Passion fruits are loaded with antioxidants that inhibit cancer growth and flavonoids that promote heart health. They also contain phenols that have antimicrobial activity. They are high in carbohydrates and simple sugars, providing an instant energy source for athletes.

cherry cornmeal cake

Cherries and corn are a natural combination because are both at their best at the same time of the year. Crunchy on the outside and smooth and moist inside, this dessert cake is a crowd pleaser.

2½ tablespoons coconut oil

100 g / 1 cup finely ground yellow cornmeal (or Italian polenta)

240 ml / 1 cup low-fat organic milk

3 eggs

120 ml / ½ cup agave nectar

1 teaspoon baking powder

½ teaspoon ground cinnamon

150 g / 1½ cups pitted sweet cherries, halved

plain Greek yogurt (0% fat), to serve (optional)

a 23-cm / 9-inch round non-stick cake pan

Serves 6

Preheat the oven to 180°C (350°F) Gas 4.

Place the cake pan in the oven for 10 minutes. Add ½ tablespoon of the coconut oil and swirl around the pan to coat its side and bottom.

Put the remaining coconut oil, cornmeal, milk, eggs, agave nectar, baking powder and cinnamon in a mixing bowl and stir together.

Add the cherries and stir in. Pour the mixture into the prepared cake pan and level the surface with a spatula.

Bake in the preheated oven for 30–35 minutes, until the cake has risen and springs back to the touch. Allow to cool in the tin set on a wire rack for 10 minutes. To serve, cut into slices and top with a dollop of Greek yogurt, if liked.

 ♥ **cornmeal** is made from whole, dried, ground corn kernels. It provides a good source of dietary fibre. Cornmeal is low in saturated fat, sodium and cholesterol. It is a gluten-free, wholesome source of carbohydrates, ideal for healthy weight gain.

apple and quince crumble

Layers of warm juicy fruit and crisp buttery dough come together in this timeless dessert. If you can't find quinces or they are out of season, replace with a different variety of apples or firm pears.

3 quinces, peeled and cut into eighths

3 crisp red apples, cut into eighths

75 g / ½ cup sultanas/ golden raisins

¼ teaspoon ground allspice

½ teaspoon ground cinnamon

¼ teaspoon sea salt

3 tablespoons almond flour or coconut flour

60 ml / ¼ cup unsweetened apple juice

Snog Natural Pure Frozen Yogurt (see page 20), to serve (optional)

crumble topping

115 g / 1 stick unsalted butter, melted

200 g / ¾ cup plain/ all-purpose gluten-free flour (such as Doves Farm or Bob's Red Mill)

60 ml / ¼ cup agave nectar

¼ teaspoon sea salt

40 g / ⅓ cup chopped pecans

a 25-cm / 8-inch square baking dish, greased

Serves 6–8

Preheat the oven to 190°C (375°F) Gas 5.

Put the quinces in a small saucepan. Cover with water, set over high heat and cook for about 10 minutes, until the fruit is tender.

Put the apples, sultanas/golden raisins, allspice, cinnamon, salt, almond flour, apple juice and cooked quince in a mixing bowl. Stir to combine, making sure you turn and coat every piece of fruit. Put the mixture in the prepared baking dish. Bake in the preheated oven for 15–20 minutes, until the juices are bubbling.

Put the butter, flour, agave nectar, salt and pecans in a large bowl. Bring together using your hands, until a sticky dough forms.

Remove the baking dish from the oven and scatter the dough randomly over the fruit. Return to the oven and bake for a further 10–15 minutes, until the crumble is golden. Allow to cool slightly before serving with a scoop of Snog Natural Pure Frozen Yogurt, if liked.

♥ **quinces** are rich in antioxidant and antiviral activity and a good source of vitamin A, dietary fibre and iron. They have powerful astringent properties, due a high tannin content and contain pectin that lowers the levels of LDL 'bad' cholesterol and help reduce the risk of heart disease.

persimmon and macadamia bread pudding

Here is a magical solution to 'what do we do with this day-old bread?' The creamy persimmon and crunchy macadamia nuts make a scrumptious combination. If you find Fuyu persimmons, use the same quantity but remember to remove the seeds.

4 ripe persimmons (Sharon fruit), peeled and diced

720 ml / 3 cups low-fat milk

3 eggs, lightly beaten

420 ml / 1¾ cups agave nectar

75 g / ½ cup chopped macadamia nuts

1 teaspoon vanilla extract

½ teaspoon ground cinnamon

⅛ teaspoon freshly ground nutmeg

400 g / 14 oz. day-old gluten-free bread, cut into 1-cm / ½-inch slices

plain Greek yogurt (0% fat), to serve (optional)

a 23 x 33-cm / 9 x 13-inch baking dish, greased

Serves 10

Put the persimmon flesh in a blender and process until puréed. Put the milk, eggs and agave nectar in a large bowl and use a hand-held electric mixer to whisk well. Add the persimmon purée, macadamias, vanilla, cinnamon and nutmeg and beat until combined. Arrange the bread slices in the prepared baking dish and pour in the persimmon mixture. Cover with clingfilm/plastic wrap and set aside for 30 minutes, to allow the bread to soak up the liquid.

Preheat the oven to 180°C (350°F) Gas 4. Bake the pudding in the preheated oven for 35–40 minutes, until golden brown and no longer wet. Allow to cool slightly and serve warm with Greek yogurt on the side, if liked.

♥ **persimmons** should be eaten when soft and fully ripe, otherwise they can be quite astringent. They have a high antioxidant content and are rich in iron, calcium, copper and vitamins C and A, and contain some manganese and potassium. Persimmons are a very good source of dietary fibre and can help heal digestive disorders.

raw food treats

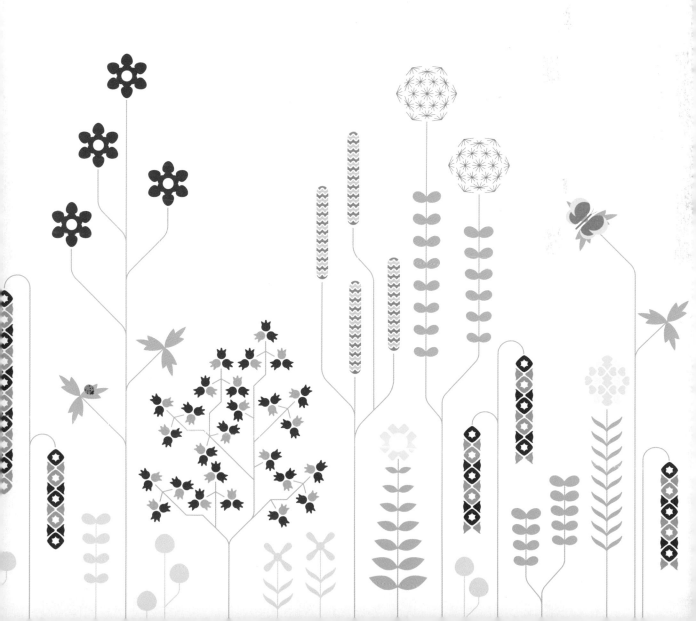

lemon cashew bars

If you like lemon bars you will love this exotic version! These beautiful treats are made from crunchy cashew nuts, chewy raisins and tangy lemons. Presoaking the cashew nuts enables them to blend more easily into a creamy topping.

base

225 g / 2 cups raw cashew nuts

¼ teaspoon sea salt

40 g / ¼ cup sultanas/golden raisins

freshly squeezed juice and grated zest of 1 lemon

2 tablespoons agave nectar

topping

100 g / 1 scant cup raw cashew nuts

80 ml / ⅓ cup freshly squeezed lemon juice

60 ml / ¼ cup agave nectar

¼ teaspoon ground turmeric

2 tablespoons coconut oil or coconut cream

1 teaspoon grated lemon zest, to decorate

a 30 x 10-cm / 12 x 4-inch loose-based flan tin, lined with parchment paper

Serves 6

To make the base, put the cashew nuts and salt in the bowl of a food processor and process until coarsely ground. Add the sultanas/golden raisins, lemon juice, agave nectar and lemon zest and process until the mixture begins to stick together and form coarse crumbs. Sprinkle the mixture in the prepared pan and distribute loosely. Use the tips of your fingers or a spatula to press down to form a base. Chill in the freezer for 20 minutes.

To make the topping, soak the cashew nuts in 480 ml / 2 cups cold water for at least 3 hours and drain well. Combine the cashew nuts, lemon juice and agave nectar in a blender and process until smooth. Add the turmeric and blend again. Add the coconut oil and blend thoroughly. Pour the topping over the chilled crust and spread evenly with a spatula.

Freeze for 2 hours and then transfer to the refrigerator. Decorate with lemon zest, cut into slices and serve chilled.

Stored in an airtight container in the refrigerator, these bars will keep for up to 4 days.

♥ **cashew nuts** are rich in nutrients as well as flavour. They are loaded with copper, magnesium, phosphorous, niacin and folate. Most of the fat in cashew nuts is monounsaturated fat (oleic acid). This fatty acid is really good for you as it can lower the levels of LDL 'bad' cholesterol. Eating cashew nuts regularly, and in moderate amounts, can help reduce the risk of heart disease and cancer.

fresh blackberry pie on spiced almond crust

This comforting pie has the wonderful taste of almonds, blackberries and warming spices, and it literally takes no time to make!

pie crust

350 g / 2 cups raw almonds

½ teaspoon sea salt

½ teaspoon ground allspice

85 g / ⅓ cup raisins

2 tablespoons agave nectar

1 tablespoon vanilla extract

filling

500 g / 4 cups fresh blackberries

8 soft Medjool dates, pitted

1 tablespoon agave nectar

1 tablespoon freshly squeezed lemon juice

plain Greek yogurt (0% fat), to serve (optional)

a 23-cm / 9-inch diameter shallow dish/pie plate

Serves 6

To make the pie crust, put the almonds, salt and allspice in the bowl of a food processor. Process until finely ground and loose. Add the raisins, agave nectar, vanilla and 1 tablespoon cold water and process until the mixture begins to stick together to form coarse crumbs.

Put the mixture in the dish/pie plate and distribute along the bottom and the sides to form an even layer. Press to compact with your hands, shaping the crust flush with the rim. (The pie crust should be about 8 mm / ⅜ inch thick.) Chill in the refrigerator for 20 minutes.

To make the filling, put 250 g / 2 cups of the blackberries, the dates, agave nectar and lemon juice in the bowl of a food processor and process until smooth. Transfer to a large bowl and stir in the remaining blackberries.

Pour the filling into the pie crust and distribute evenly with a spatula. Refrigerate for 2 hours then cut into slices and serve chilled with Greek yogurt on the side, if liked.

Stored in an airtight container in the refrigerator, this pie will keep for 4 days.

♥ **almonds** contain vitamins A and E, which are responsible for enhancing our skin's health and protecting it from sun damage. They are rich in monounsaturated fat, which lowers LDL 'bad' cholesterol and helps reduce the risk of heart disease. Almonds are a rich source of protein and dietary fibre, which can that help us lose weight when eaten in moderation.

mango coconut macadamia torte

This recipe is inspired by my favourite tropical flavours: coconut and mango. The torte is surprisingly moist and it's like a bite of island paradise for coconut lovers.

torte base

250 g / 2 cups shelled macadamia nuts

100 g / 1 cup unsweetened shredded dried coconut

¼ teaspoon sea salt

16 soft Medjool dates, pitted and roughly chopped

2 teaspoons vanilla extract

mango topping

325 g / 12 oz. peeled and cubed ripe mango, plus extra slices, to decorate

3 tablespoons agave nectar

2 teaspoons powdered soya / soy lecithin

3 tablespoons coconut oil

175 g / 6 oz. raspberries

a 23-cm / 9-inch springform cake pan

Serves 8–10

Put the macadamias, coconut and salt in the bowl of a food processor and process until finely ground and loose. Add the dates and vanilla and process until the mixture begins to stick together and form coarse crumbs. Add 2 tablespoons cold water and process again until well mixed. Transfer the mixture to the cake pan and press to compact with a spatula or back of a large spoon. Chill in the refrigerator for 20 minutes.

Put the cubed mango and agave nectar in a blender and purée until smooth. Add the soya lecithin and process again. Pour in the coconut oil while the motor is running and process until the mixture is very smooth.

Spread the mango mixture over the chilled torte base, using a spatula to level the surface. Cover with clingfilm/plastic wrap and refrigerate for 4 hours. Garnish with slices of mango and fresh raspberries and serve chilled.

Covered with clingfilm/plastic wrap in the refrigerator, this torte will keep for 4 days.

♥ **coconut** is one of the healthiest oils available. It is a medium chain fatty acid that our body quickly metabolizes into an energy source rather than store it around our hips or stomach. This fat contains lauric acid: an antiviral, antimicrobial and antibacterial agent. Coconut and its oil are rich in nutrients, while the coconut water has the perfect balance of electrolytes, enzymes and vitamins.

cacao-pecan bars with creamy frosting

This recipe is for all chocolate lovers, so that they can turn their cravings into good nutrition. Cacao is one of nature's most fantastic superfoods with the highest antioxidant value. In this recipe, even the creamy frosting has a healthy surprise!

pecan bars

225 g / 8 oz. raw pecans

50 g / 2 oz. raw cacao powder or good quality cocoa powder

⅛ teaspoon sea salt

10 soft Medjool dates, pitted

60 ml / ¼ cup agave nectar

cacao avocado frosting

4 soft Medjool dates, pitted

1 medium Hass avocado

25 g / 1 oz. raw cacao powder or good-quality cocoa powder

60 ml / ¼ cup agave nectar

30 g / 1 oz. pecan nuts, roughly chopped, to decorate

a 30 x 10-cm / 12 x 4-inch loose-based flan pan, lined with parchment paper

Serves 6

To make the bars, put the pecans, cacao powder and salt in the bowl of a food processor. Process until finely ground and loose. Add the dates and agave nectar and process until the mixture begins to stick together and forms coarse crumbs.

Sprinkle the mixture into the prepared pan and distribute loosely. Press evenly to compact using a spatula. Chill in the refrigerator for 20 minutes.

To make the frosting, cover the dates with cold water and soak for 20 minutes. Drain the dates and put them in the bowl of a food processor along with the avocado, cacao powder and agave nectar and process until smooth. Stop occasionally to scrape down the sides of the bowl with a spatula and process again until very smooth.

Spread the frosting evenly on top of the pecan bars and scatter with chopped pecans. Refrigerate for 2 hours, then cut into slices and serve chilled.

Stored in an airtight container in the refrigerator, these bars will keep for 4 days.

♥ **dates** are nature's sweet candy and a great source of quick energy. They are rich in calcium, magnesium, potassium and iron. Dates contain tannins and other antioxidants that have anti-cancer and anti-inflammatory properties. Dates are the perfect sweetener for many recipes. They are a healthier alternative to processed or refined sugars and they are a great source of dietary fibre.

pistachio and pineapple yogurt crumble

This recipe is inspired by Pablo's sister Xandy's favourite dessert and is where the whole idea for Snog began. A healthy treat that consists of a nut crumble topped with yogurt and fresh fruit. Imagine the possibilities!

325 g / 13 oz. finely chopped fresh pineapple

175 g / 6 oz. fresh raspberries

60 ml / ¼ cup agave nectar

1 tablespoon finely chopped fresh mint leaves

200 g / 1 cup shelled raw pistachio nuts

¼ teaspoon sea salt

8 soft Medjool dates, pitted

1 teaspoon vanilla extract

480 ml / 2 cups plain Greek yogurt (0% or 2% fat)

extra agave nectar, to taste

Serves 6–8

Combine the pineapple, raspberries, agave nectar and mint in a bowl and toss lightly. Cover and allow to marinate for at least 15 minutes.

Put the pistachios and salt in the bowl of a food processor and process lightly. Add the dates, vanilla and 1 tablespoon cold water and process until the mixture begins to stick together to form coarse crumbs. Divide most of the mixture between 6–8 serving dishes and top with the yogurt and the pineapple and raspberry marinade. (Drizzle with extra agave nectar if you prefer a sweeter dessert.) Scatter the remaining crumble mixture over the top and serve.

Stored separately in airtight containers in the refrigerator, the fruit marinade and pistachio crumble will keep for 3 days.

♥ **pineapple** contains bromelain, a powerful enzyme compound. It is a natural anti-inflammatory that helps reduce swelling, aids in digestion and boosts the immune system. Pineapples are also a natural blood thinner. They are rich in vitamin C and manganese, which promotes healthy skin and bones.

mojito mousse on coconut crunch

This recipe is inspired by the sweetness, refreshing citrus and spearmint flavours in the Cuban Mojito cocktail, a popular summer drink. Most people are not used to eating avocados for dessert, since they don't regard it as a fruit. I enjoy sharing this dessert with others – it's always popular and very refreshing!

coconut crunch

100 g / 4 oz. raw walnuts

100 g / 4 oz. unsweetened shredded dried coconut

¼ teaspoon sea salt

4 soft Medjool dates, pitted and roughly chopped

1 tablespoon agave nectar

mojito mousse

2 Hass avocados

240 ml / 1 cup freshly squeezed lime juice

180 ml / ¾ cup agave nectar

30 g / 1 oz. fresh spearmint leaves, plus a few extra to decorate

2 tablespoons coconut oil or coconut cream

Serves 6

Put the walnuts, coconut and salt in the bowl of a food processor. Process until finely ground and loose but do not overprocess as nuts can easily become a creamy butter. (It is better to process a little at a time and check for consistency.)

Add the dates and agave nectar and process until the mixture begins to stick together and form coarse crumbs. Sprinkle the mixture into 6 serving dishes. Press to compact with your fingertips. Chill in the refrigerator for 20 minutes.

To make the mojito mousse, put the avocados, lime juice, agave nectar and spearmint in the bowl of a food processor and process until smooth. You may have to stop and scrape down the sides of the bowl a few times. Pour in the coconut oil while the motor is running and process until it is incorporated and very smooth.

Distribute the mousse evenly between the dishes. Cover well with clingfilm/plastic wrap and refrigerate for 3 hours. Decorate with spearmint leaves and serve chilled.

Covered with clingfilm/plastic wrap and stored in the refrigerator, this dessert will keep for 3 days.

♥ **avocado** is nature's healthy cream; a monounsaturated fat, that actually lowers LDL 'bad' cholesterol, helps our heart and keeps our skin moist. They are a great source of fibre and potassium. Avocados also contain folate, vitamin A and other healthy carotenoids. They promote optimal health while increasing the body's ability to absorb vital nutrients.

apricot cashew cobbler

This fresh-tasting cobbler will make you fall in love with fresh apricots. The delicate compote spooned over a crunchy cashew nut base is a healthy choice and a personal favourite. You can even enjoy this for breakfast.

base

300 g / 10 oz. raw cashew nuts

¼ teaspoon sea salt

2 tablespoons agave nectar

1 teaspoon vanilla extract

apricot compote

9 ripe apricots, pitted

70 g / 3 oz. dried apricots

60 ml / ¼ cup agave nectar

1 tablespoon freshly squeezed lemon juice

Serves 6–8

Put the cashews and salt in the bowl of a food processor and chop coarsely. Add the agave nectar and vanilla and pulse lightly. Put in a bowl and chill in the refrigerator for 20 minutes.

Put 6 of the fresh apricots, the dried apricots, agave nectar and lemon juice in the bowl of a food processor and process until smooth. Slice the remaining fresh apricots and set aside.

Divide most of the mixture between 6–8 serving dishes. Top with apricot compote and fresh apricot slices. Scatter the remaining cashew mixture on top and serve immediately.

Stored separately in airtight containers in the refrigerator, the apricot compote and cashew nut mixture will keep for 4 days.

♥ **apricots** are rich in fibre, potassium, vitamin A and betacarotene. They also contain beta-cryptoxanthin, a potent antioxidant that can help reduce the risk of lung and colon cancer. Apricots are low in calories and rich in nutrients. They promote healthy hair and radiant skin.

saffron yogurt parfait

Hand-picked saffron is the most delicate spice in the world. I love the 'perfect' flavour and the colour it gives to this decadent yogurt parfait!

¼ teaspoon saffron threads

2 tablespoons hot water

480 ml / 2 cups plain Greek yogurt (0% or 2% fat)

60 ml / ¼ cup agave nectar

225 g / 1½ cups raw pecans

130 g / 5 oz. dried Bing cherries or other tart variety

325 g / 2 cups finely cubed fresh mango

Serves 6–8

Dissolve the saffron threads in the hot water. Set aside for 1 hour. Strain through a fine sieve and discard the saffron threads. Combine the saffron-infused water with the yogurt and agave nectar, mixing thoroughly. Chill in the refrigerator for 1 hour.

Put the pecans and cherries in the bowl of a food processor and process to form coarse crumbs.

Divide half of the mixture between 6–8 serving dishes. Top with a layer of the saffron yogurt and a layer of fresh mango. Scatter the remaining crumble mixture on top and serve immediately.

Stored separately in airtight containers in the refrigerator, the saffron yogurt and pecan crumble will keep for 5 days.

❤ **mangoes** are a rich source of enzymes. They supply fibre, help treat acidity and relieve constipation. Mangoes are loaded with potassium, betacarotene and vitamins A and C. They also contain phenols, which have anticancer and antioxidant properties. Mangoes are high in iron, making them ideal for pregnant women and those with anaemia.

pear ginger carpaccio

This is a very refreshing and light dessert. The recipe is suitable for any kind of pear and pretty much for any other variety of fruit that you can slice paper thin.

2 ripe pears, cored and very thinly sliced

2 tablespoons agave nectar

¼ teaspoon finely grated fresh ginger

4 strawberries, halved, to decorate

2 tablespoons finely chopped pistachio nuts

Serves 4

Arrange the pear slices in one layer on a large plate or in a shallow dish.

Put the agave nectar and ginger in a small bowl and whisk thoroughly, until combined. Drizzle this mixture over the pear slices. Cover tightly with clingfilm/plastic wrap and chill in the refrigerator for 30 minutes.

When ready to serve, divide the pear slices between 4 serving plates, decorate with strawberry halves and sprinkle with chopped pistachio nuts.

Stored in an airtight container in the refrigerator, the pear slices in syrup will keep for 3 days.

♥ **pears** have a very high fibre content and are beneficial for colonic health. They are a good source of vitamin C and copper and provide antioxidant activity. Pears are rich in potassium and contain calcium, phosphorous and magnesium. They are recommended as a hypoallergenic food, ideal for introducing infants to fruit.

chocolate raspberry bites

These healthy yet delicious chocolate bites are a little chewy brownie topped with a juicy and delicate fresh raspberry. They are very easy to make and perfect for serving at the end of a dinner party.

300 g / 10 oz. walnuts

50 g / 2 oz. raw cacao powder or good-quality cocoa powder

⅛ teaspoon sea salt

10 soft Medjool dates, pitted

60 ml / ¼ cup agave nectar

1 teaspoon vanilla extract

250 g / 9 oz. fresh raspberries

Serves 6–8 (makes about 30–36 bites)

Put the walnuts, cacao powder and salt in the bowl of a food processor. Process until finely ground and loose.

Add the dates, agave nectar and vanilla and process until the mixture begins to stick together. Wet your hands and roll the mixture into 2.5-cm / 1-inch balls. Indent a thumbprint on top of each ball and place a fresh raspberry in the centre. Chill in the refrigerator for 20 minutes before serving.

Stored in an airtight container in the refrigerator, these bites will keep for 3 days.

♥ **walnuts** are a great source of omega-3s. They regulate brain function and promote healthy mood balance. They are rich in minerals such as calcium, magnesium, manganese and potassium. Walnuts are also a rich source of protein and dietary fibre, which helps us lose weight when eaten in moderation.

pistachio apricot truffles

Pistachios and apricots are a perfect match. This recipe is always a favourite, it's fun to make and 15 minutes is all it takes!

200 g / 7 oz. shelled unsalted pistachio nuts

350 g / 12 oz. dried apricots

2 tablespoons freshly squeezed lime juice

2 tablespoons agave nectar

Serves 6–8 (makes about 30 truffles)

Very finely chop 50 g / 2 oz. of the pistachios and set aside until needed.

Put the apricots, lime juice and agave nectar in the bowl of a food processor and process until smooth. Add the remaining pistachios and pulse to chop the nuts very lightly and mix. Wet your hands and roll the mixture into 2.5-cm / 1-inch balls.

Roll the truffles in the chopped pistachio nuts and set in a plate. Chill in the refrigerator for 2 hours before serving.

Covered with clingfilm/plastic wrap in the refrigerator, these truffles will keep for 5 days.

fig almond truffles

These truffles are a quick healthy snack any time of day. I like to eat them in the afternoon for an instant energy boost.

250 g / 9 oz. raw almonds

⅛ teaspoon sea salt

1 teaspoon ground cinnamon

250 g / 9 oz. dried black mission figs, chopped

2 tablespoons freshly squeezed orange juice

60 ml / ¼ cup agave nectar

85 g / 3 oz. dried cranberries

Serves 6–8 (makes about 30–36 truffles)

Very finely chop 50 g / 2 oz. of the almonds and set aside until needed.

Put the remaining almonds, salt and cinnamon in the bowl of a food processor and process into small pieces. Add the figs, orange juice and agave nectar and process until the mixture begins to stick together. Add the cranberries and pulse to mix. Wet your hands and roll the mixture into 2.5-cm / 1-inch balls.

Roll the truffles in the chopped almonds to coat. Chill in the refrigerator for 2 hours before serving.

Stored in an airtight container in the refrigerator, these truffles will keep for 5 days.

smoothies & drinks

chocolatey blueberry pomegranate smoothie

Pomegranates are not only very good for you, but also a visual delight with their jewel-like seeds. Decorating your drink with a few of these fresh seeds can make your morning even smoother.

230 g / 2 cups fresh blueberries

360 ml / 1½ cups plain Greek yogurt (0% fat)

80 ml / ⅓ cup unsweetened pomegranate juice

2 tablespoons good-quality cocoa powder

1 teaspoon agave nectar

2 teaspoons almond butter

300 g / 10 oz. ice cubes, crushed (see note)

extra blueberries or pomegranate seeds, to decorate (optional)

Serves 4

Put the blueberries, yogurt, pomegranate juice, cocoa, agave nectar and almond butter in a blender and process until puréed and smooth.

Just before serving, add the crushed ice and process again until frothy. Pour into tall glasses, garnish with a few fresh blueberries or pomegranate seeds, as preferred, and serve immediately.

Note: Most blenders can crush ice. If you have a food processor and not a blender it may not be possible to crush ice in it; check the manufacturer's instructions. Alternatively you can put the ice cubes in a polythene bag and crush them by hitting them with a rolling pin.

♥ **blueberries** are considered excellent brain and memory food. They help neurons in the brain function more effectively and keep our memory sharp. Blueberries are rich in antioxidant and anti-inflammatory properties, helping those with arthritis and heart disease. Blueberries also rank high in anticancer activity.

coconut ginger smoothie

There's nothing like this warming and energizing smoothie to get you up and out on a chilly morning. Rich and satisfying, it's great for breakfast on the go or served as a mid-afternoon pick-me-up.

240 ml / 1 cup light coconut milk

240 ml plain Greek yogurt (0% fat)

2 bananas, cut into chunks

3 tablespoons agave nectar

3 tablespoons freshly squeezed lime juice

1 tablespoon ginger juice or 15 g / ½ oz. peeled and grated fresh ginger

200 g / 7 oz. ice cubes, crushed (see note)

ground ginger or slivers of desiccated ginger, to decorate

Serves 4

Put the coconut milk, yogurt, banana chunks, agave nectar, lime juice and ginger juice or grated ginger in a blender and process until smooth. Add the crushed ice and pulse a few times until frothy.

Pour into 4 glass tumblers and decorate with a light sprinkling of ground ginger or a pinch of desiccated ginger, as preferred, and serve immediately.

Note: Most blenders can crush ice. If you have a food processor and not a blender it may not be possible to crush ice in it; check the manufacturer's instructions. Alternatively you can put the ice cubes in a polythene bag and crush them by hitting them with a rolling pin.

♥ **ginger** has been used to aid an upset stomach and relieve nausea since ancient times, as it stimulates saliva and helps digestion. It can be a great help to pregnant women suffering from morning sickness. It is loaded with antioxidants, some of which have anti-inflammatory properties. Ginger also improves circulation and generates heat within our bodies.

minty raspberry nectarine smoothie

One summer, I picked raspberries at my friend's backyard. We swam in the lake nearby and for dinner we had raspberries, yogurt and mint (also from his garden). I will never forget the experience of tasting those three ingredients together. They kindle sweet memories of blooming flavours.

120 g / 1 cup frozen raspberries

2 fresh nectarines, pitted and quartered

85 g / 1 cup Snog Natural Pure Frozen Yogurt (see page 20)

480 ml / 2 cups nectarine or apricot nectar (see note)

2 tablespoons finely chopped fresh mint

a few extra raspberries and 4 nectarine slices, to decorate

Serves 4

Put the raspberries, nectarines, frozen yogurt, nectarine or apricot nectar and mint in a blender and process until puréed and smooth.

Pour into 4 glass tumblers, decorate with raspberries and nectarine slices and serve immediately.

Note: Nectarine or apricot nectar is thicker than the juice and is sold in bottles or cans. It's most often found in health food stores or organic markets, but can be found in larger supermarkets.

♥ **raspberries** are extremely high in dietary fibre. They are rich in calcium, magnesium, phosphorous, potassium and vitamin C. They contain ellagic acid, which fights cancer cells without damaging any of the healthy cells. Raspberries also contain anthocyanin, a potent antioxidant with anti-inflammatory properties.

papaya lassi

The first time I tasted a lassi, I couldn't believe the exhilarating effect of salt and ripe fruit. I started experimenting with all types of fruit but my ultimate favourite is still papaya, the first one I ever tasted.

2 fresh papayas, peeled and diced

720 ml / 3 cups plain Greek yogurt (2% fat)

10 g / ½ cup fresh mint leaves

½ teaspoon freshly ground black pepper

¼ teaspoon sea salt

ice cubes, to serve

a few fresh mint sprigs, to decorate

Serves 4

Put the papaya, yogurt, mint, black pepper and salt in a blender and add 500 ml / 2 cups cold water. Process until puréed and smooth.

Pour into 4 tall glasses filled with ice cubes. Garnish with fresh mint sprigs and serve immediately.

♥ papayas are loaded with digestive enzymes. They contain papain, an enzyme that helps digest protein and has anti-inflammatory properties. Papayas are also a rich source of antioxidants such as carotene, vitamin C and flavonoids, as well as potassium and dietary fibre.

iced almond chai

Making your own chai mix is a bit of an eccentricity, I know, as it is readily available. But grinding the spices yourself and experiencing the richness of their scent almost takes you to an Indian market. I usually make a double batch of the spice mix to keep handy for a later craving.

12 cardamom pods, seeded or ¼ teaspoon ground cardamom

a 5-cm / 2-inch piece of cinnamon stick, broken up

8 allspice berries

720 ml / 3 cups almond milk

2 teaspoons agave nectar

1 teaspoon finely grated fresh ginger

360 ml / 1½ cups boiling water

2 tea bags (black)

ice cubes, to serve

4 cinnamon sticks, to decorate (optional)

a spice grinder or pestle and mortar

Serves 4

Put the cardamom seeds, cinnamon and allspice in a spice grinder and process to a fine powder or use a pestle and mortar.

Put the almond milk, agave nectar, grated ginger and ground spices in a saucepan and set over medium heat. Warm gently, without letting the mixture come to the boil. Remove from the heat, cover and let stand for 15 minutes.

Meanwhile, pour the boiling water over the tea bags. Let steep for 10 minutes then strain and chill in the refrigerator.

Combine the chilled tea and spiced almond milk, taste for sweetness and add a little more agave nectar if necessary. Pour into 4 tall glasses filled with ice, decorate each with a cinnamon stick and serve immediately.

♥ **cardamom** has been used as a digestive aid since ancient times. It helps prevent stomach cramps by stimulating digestion, reducing mucus and relieving gas. Cardamom stimulates liver health by maintaining proper bile flow. It contains limonene, which provides antioxidant and detoxifying activity. Cardamom seeds are also a fantastic natural breath freshener.

tangy green juice

We have all heard about the health benefits of drinking green juice. The usual recipes use sophisticated juicers and other equipment. Here is our own simple version of a healthy drink with all the green power we need.

1 crisp green apple, peeled, cored and diced

2 fresh kiwi fruit, peeled and sliced

225 g / 1 cup cubed ripe honeydew melon

60 ml / ¼ cup agave nectar

3 tablespoons freshly squeezed lime juice

¼ teaspoon cayenne pepper

ice cubes, to serve

Serves 4

Put the apple, kiwi fruit, melon, agave nectar, lime juice and cayenne in a blender and add 360 ml / 1½ cups cold water. Process until puréed and smooth.

Pour into 4 tall ice-filled glasses and serve immediately.

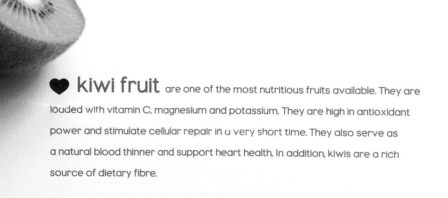

♥ **kiwi fruit** are one of the most nutritious fruits available. They are loaded with vitamin C, magnesium and potassium. They are high in antioxidant power and stimulate cellular repair in a very short time. They also serve as a natural blood thinner and support heart health. In addition, kiwis are a rich source of dietary fibre.

cranberry and lemon 'punch'

This is a refreshing and soothing drink that evokes the 1950s favourite, but minus the cloying sweet syrupy flavour and plus the citrusy and bubbly sorbet.

640 ml / 2⅔ cups unsweetened cranberry juice

4 scoops lemon sorbet (about 40 g / 1½ oz. each)

240 ml / 1 cup soda water or sparkling mineral water

lemon slices, to decorate

ice cubes, to serve

Serves 4

Fill 4 tall glasses with ice cubes. Divide the cranberry juice between them.

Add one scoop of the lemon sorbet to each glass and top up with soda water. Decorate with lemon slices and serve immediately.

♥ **cranberry juice** is extremely rich in plant nutrients that support the body's natural detoxification process. It has a very high phenol content, which helps neutralize harmful free radicals. Cranberries have very potent antioxidants. They have cancer-fighting properties and contain antibacterial agents that help prevent urinary tract infections.

grapefruit rose fizz

The stereotypical feminine drink is labelled as sweet and cloying. Here is my interpretation of a sophisticated, delicate and altogether delightful pink drink.

960 ml / 4 cups ruby red grapefruit juice, chilled

2 teaspoons rose-flower water, chilled

1 teaspoon agave nectar

1 ruby red grapefruit

240 ml / 1 cup soda water or sparkling mineral water

Serves 8

Combine the grapefruit juice, rose-flower water and agave nectar in a large jug/pitcher.

Peel the grapefruit, remove the pith and divide the flesh into segments. Cut each segments in half.

Divide the grapefruit pulp between 8 champagne flutes (or similar), top up with the grapefruit rose juice and finish with a splash of soda water. Serve immediately.

♥ **grapefruits** are packed with enzymes, potassium, folic acid and vitamin C. They are a low-calorie, high-volume food ideal for weight loss. Grapefruit juice helps inhibits the development of cancer and lower LDL 'bad' cholesterol levels. Red and pink grapefruits have stronger antioxidant properties than white grapefruits. They also contain cancer-fighting lycopene, vitamin A and betacarotene.

orange 'agua fresca' with beet swirl

Street food is often a great source of inspiration for new flavours. I had a similar agua fresca at a Mexican market years ago and the sweetness of the beetroot combined with the fresh fruit juice was dazzling. I couldn't resist including my own version of this memorable drink here.

1 small red beetroot/beet, washed and trimmed

700 ml / 3 cups freshly squeezed orange juice

1 orange, peeled, sliced, and seeded

60 ml / ¼ cup freshly squeezed lemon juice

4 tablespoons agave nectar

2 tablespoons finely grated orange zest

ice cubes, to serve

Serves 4

Preheat the oven to 200°C (400°F) Gas 6.

Put the beetroot on a square of foil. Wrap and transfer to a baking sheet. Roast in the preheated oven for about 40 minutes, until tender when pierced with a knife. Unwrap and allow to cool. When cold enough to handle, remove the outer skin, cut the flesh into small pieces and set aside.

Put the orange juice, orange slices, lemon juice, and 3 tablespoons of the agave nectar in a blender. Add 360 ml / 1½ cups cold water and process until puréed and smooth.

Chill the orange blend in the refrigerator until very cold. Put the chopped beetroot in a blender with the orange zest, remaining agave nectar and 120 ml / ½ cup cold water and process until puréed and smooth.

To serve, pour the orange agua fresca into 4 tall ice-filled glasses and spoon 1 tablespoon of the beetroot purée on top of each drink. Serve immediately.

💜 **beetroots** are considered an excellent liver tonic and blood purifier. Betacyanin – the pigment that gives the beetroot its red colour, is a potent cancer-fighting agent. They are a good source of betaine and folate and rich in potassium, a vital mineral for heart health. They also contain iron, magnesium and vitamin C.

passion fruit mango kombucha

Kombucha is a Chinese carbonated tea, which is not only delicious and fulfilling, but also said to have great cleansing and immunological qualities. For those who stay away from soda but some times crave it, it is a wonderful alternative.

480 ml / 2 cups mango juice, chilled

120 ml / ½ cup passion fruit juice, chilled

480 ml / 2 cups natural flavoured kombucha, chilled (see note)

3 tablespoons agave nectar

ice cubes, to serve

Serves 6

Put the mango juice, passion fruit juice, kombucha and agave nectar in a large jug/pitcher and stir to combine. Pour into 6 ice-filled glasses and serve immediately.

Note: If you cannot find Kombucha you can substitute sparkling mineral water or a carbonated health drink, the type sold in health food shops. A Kombucha cordial is available in larger supermarkets, which has to be diluted with sparkling water. It contains some fruit flavourings but works well in this recipe.

❤ **kombucha** is a fermented tea that contains live cultures and provides numerous health benefits. Kombucha tea is rich in antioxidants and probiotic acids. These help strengthen the immune system, prevent cancer, detoxify the liver and aid digestion. It is also a good source of vitamin B. The ancient Chinese referred to it as the 'immortal health elixir'.

green mango and coconut slushie

Green mango is enjoyed all over the tropics. Its flavour is quite different from the ripe fruit in that it is almost savoury and on hot days actually much more refreshing. This recipe works just as well with ripe mangoes – just reduce the quantity of agave nectar by a tablespoonful or two, so as not to make it too sweet.

230 g / 2 cups diced unripe mango (or ripe if preferred)

720 ml / 3 cups canned unsweetened coconut juice

freshly squeezed juice of 1 lime

80 ml / ⅓ cup agave nectar

2 teaspoons sea salt

⅛ teaspoon cayenne pepper

coconut shavings, to decorate (optional)

a 23 x 33-cm / 9 x 13-inch metal pan (at least 2.5 cm / 1 inch deep)

Serves 4

Put the diced mango, coconut juice, lime juice, agave nectar, salt and cayenne pepper in a blender and process until puréed and smooth.

Pour into the pan and freeze for at least 2 hours. Remove from the freezer and leave at room temperature for 10 minutes then break the frozen mixture into chunks. Use a fork or beaters to whisk until soft and slushy.

Spoon into tall glasses, garnish with coconut shavings, if using, and serve immediately.

♥ **cayenne pepper** warms the body and stimulates the stomach lining to secrete powerful protective juices. It helps rebuild the stomach's tissue and assists the healing of stomach and intestinal ulcers. Cayenne pepper helps reduce high blood pressure to normal levels while cleaning the arteries and lowering LDL 'bad' cholesterol. Cayenne is widely used for its detoxifying properties.

strawberry rhubarb basil frappé

Although this combination of fruit usually comes in the form of a pie or crumble, this drink provides a lighter take that watermarks the strawberry notes.

2 large rhubarb stalks (about 70 g / 2 oz.), cut into 2.5-cm / 1-inch pieces

5 tablespoons agave nectar

280 g / 10 oz. strawberries

2 tablespoons finely chopped fresh basil

300 g / 10 oz. ice cubes, crushed (see note)

small strawberries, halved, to decorate

fresh basil leaves, to decorate

Serves 4

Put the rhubarb pieces, 2 tablespoons of the agave nectar and 120 ml / ½ cup cold water in a saucepan and set over medium heat. Bring to the boil and cook for 5 minutes, until all the water has evaporated, the agave begins to caramelize and the rhubarb is mushy. Transfer to a bowl, allow to cool and then chill in the refrigerator.

Put the strawberries, chopped basil, remaining agave nectar, crushed ice and cooked rhubarb in a blender and process until blended and frothy.

Pour into 4 glass tumblers, decorate each with a strawberry half and a few basil leaves and serve immediately.

Note: Most blenders can crush ice. If you have a food processor and not a blender it may not be possible to crush ice in it; check the manufacturer's instructions. Alternatively you can put the ice cubes in a polythene bag and crush them by hitting them with a rolling pin.

♥ **strawberries** contain chemicals that protect cells against cervical and breast cancer. They contain ellagic acid and have potent antioxidant properties. Strawberries are a rich source of vitamin C and dietary fibre. Compounds in strawberries protect our blood vessels and can help improve short-term memory.

index

acknowledgements

Pablo Uribe and Rob Baines wish to thank the following people:

Lorraine Perretta, the nutritionist who confirmed the motto 'you are what you eat' as our whole philosophy is based around how healthy eating plays a role in our physical, mental and spiritual well-being.

Xandy, as Snog Pure Frozen Yogurt is sweetened with agave nectar thanks to her.

Ico Design Consultancy for creating the Snog brand and logo we and our loyal customers love.

Cinimod Studio for giving us beautifully-lit and inspiring Snog shops.

Our Snog shop managers, Mia in Westfield, Andres in Soho and Matt in South Kensington for keeping the wheels in motion with endless smiles.

To our best friends Nonnie, Mark and Paul for being with us from day one, for listening to us talk about Snog 24/7 and for trying countless recipes.

Claire, for being a visionary, equanimous and always there.

Tristan at the Covent Garden shop, for his energy, quest for perfection and trust.

Imran from R Holding, our partner in our first international Snog shop in Dubai.

Alison, Leslie, Steve and Julia at Ryland Peters & Small, for making this book happen, for being concise, having insight and tons of experience.

Kate our wonderful photographer who makes sure everything looks as good as it tastes.

Jane and her team at Not Just Food who patiently tried and tested all the recipes.

Mariana and Cristina, the heart and soul of the Snog *Healthy Treats Cookbook*, for their inspiring and delicious recipes.

Ryland Peters & Small would like to thank Linda Bloomfield for the kind loan of plates and bowls on pages 25, 53, 71 and 104. Visit her website at www.lindabloomfield.co.uk for details.